# BLITZ THEORY

2nd Edition

# BLITZ THEORY

2nd Edition

JONATHAN MAXWELL

Silent Lyric Productions, Inc.

Silent Lyric Productions, Inc.
200 Fogg Mountain Lane
Flint Hill, VA 22627

First published 1999
2nd edition published 2005


Front cover photography by Jonathan Maxwell
Back cover photography by Frank Murray
Typeset and Proofing by Kit Kat Maxwell
Printed in the US by Technical Communication Services
Distributed by Biblio Distribution
ISBN 0-9677752-0-5

# CONTENTS

Dedicated to Greg Brown and Blake Goodwin
for letting me learn the hard way.

# FORWARD

We are a playful species. From our earliest childhood we indulge in all sorts of games, but those of us who not only play but want or even must be intellectually challenged compete at the greatest game ever devised called chess.

Without doubt the fastest, most exciting roller-coaster, spine-tingling form of chess is *blitz*. We get a decision in under ten minutes, and play whole events in only one to three hours! While many kids can be daunted by the unfair stereotype of chess as a slow, laborious undertaking, blitz reveals to them just how much fun chess can be as they experience first-hand this training time control utilized by even the formidable Russians and Icelanders. While regular chess requires a lot of pondering, suffering, and preparation, blitz is a physical as well as mental game contested with intuition, speed, and just plain determination. Perhaps it is best summed up as a one-on-one, twenty-first century equivalent of a shoot-out at the O.K. Corral!

Through a revolutionary appreciation of the clock, Blitz Theory yields excellent strategies, insightful tactical options, and effective techniques for dealing with desperate situations. If in slow chess the king is Commander in Chief, then in blitz the clock is God who punishes the sin of slow playing with the holiest of wraths! Of course there are some that only play for speed, but the top players of the twentieth century like Fine,

Najdorf, Petrosian, Fischer, Karpov, Kasparov, Dlugy, Seriwan, and Tal made an effort to play both strongly and quickly. It is a method for cultivating this such strength with speed that lies in the following pages.

My personal formula for success has been to play very fast for the first fifteen to twenty moves, and then play at a comfortable pace of about one move every three seconds. Falling behind over a minute usually spells disaster. I believe one's optimum pace depends on his individual endgame technique, and plain speed in the last minute.

I agree wholeheartedly with Jonathan that a sharp opening is pivotal against non-masters. The weaker the opposition, the more effective a thoughtful opening will be; however, the slow chess maxim holds true in blitz that it is most important to play openings which one knows and with which one feels comfortable.

The only place where the WBCA draws the line concerns the "pseudo check" technique. This may be OK at coffeehouses, but will garner a penalty in WBCA events! Otherwise I endorse this uniquely insightful book with open arms!

-*Walter Browne*
Six-time U.S. Champion

# PREFACE

Before presenting the material, a few things must be stated.

Firstly, this is a tome of strategies that transforms the competitive standard chess player into a competitive blitz player. This implies that the reader is familiar with basic chess theory. *If he isn't, then he must first study this theory or this book will not help him.* While blitz is indeed its own discipline, its piece mechanics are the same as that of standard chess (which we will refer to as "slow chess"), so in the most fundamental sense the blitz game still operates along the same principles. Standard concepts such as center control, piece development, and pressuring pins are every bit as important in blitz as in slow chess, and it is only from this fundamental framework that one can build his new and varied blitz skills. Like trying to build a balcony before first erecting a foyer, learning blitz before slow chess is equally fatuous.

Secondly, the following ideas are sound at any level of blitz play; however, they are most effective for players not yet at the master level. One who plays at a WBCA level above 2200 is so intimate with the mechanics of slow chess that he will not be significantly affected by many of the following strategies. This player has "mastered" his understanding and technique to the point that the time crisis has little consequence when compared to the logic of the board. He can calculate at the blink of an eye, and has experienced every type of position so many times that he can derive the best plan instantly. This being the case, the usually towering mental, psychological, and emotional factors inherent in a normal blitz contest are now trivial when discussing a master. He may use an isolated blitz tactic on occasion, but at his level there really is no such thing as true blitz chess. For him five minutes is an iceage.

Finally, it is true that many of the following concepts contradict antiquated logic. Because of these contradictions, traditional minds may refuse to challenge certain timeworn principles, and dismiss different revolutionary ideas found in this book. No doubt, there will be many who will champion obvious mundane chess logic with statements such as "The best move is only a consequence of the position of the pieces." or "Deliberately hanging a piece is foolish." To these arguments I can only refer to the premise of the book that "slow" chess and "blitz" chess are not the same discipline. If one refuses to accept this then he cannot benefit from the text.

The fact is that blitz chess is indeed an altogether different game, and must be seen as such if one is to gain the optimum skills for success. This conclusion is not a mere derivation of an unbridled imagination; on the contrary, it is the empirical verdict from mastering the discipline through playing thousands upon thousands of blitz games. While the mechanics of slow chess and blitz chess are the same, blitz theory is unique and overwhelmingly relevant. To not appreciate this is strategically irresponsible and naive.

# INTRODUCTION

## *Blitz Chess Is Not Chess*

The game of slow chess is a discipline of crystalline logic. The contestant assesses each new position and selects the move he believes best remedies the sum of the many varied considerations before him. The victor is then the one who has most astutely manipulated the total of these positions. In this challenge there are no external factors. Only the logic dominates. That's it.

The game of blitz chess is only a relative of slow chess as *Blitz is chess within a time crisis.* This cannot be stated enough. Only when we understand this fact can we begin to appreciate what it takes to be competitive blitz players. Many see blitz as simply a fast game of chess. This is incorrect, for this implies that the best move in blitz is the same as that of slow chess. While in slow chess the situation is always dictated by the board, in blitz both the board and the clock dictate the advantage. While the gain of a piece is usually decisive in slow chess, it is often far from decisive in blitz as a flag violation deems the board status inconsequential. The details of the contest are meaningless if weighed without this fact.

In the purely logical medium of slow chess, masterful technique is realized through appreciating the varied and subtle, and executing with inspired delicacy and precision. This practice is known as "the artists touch", and its cultivation can often supersede a competitor's desire to win.

In blitz, however, there is no room for untempered artistry as the time crisis directly forbids it. If we attempt to find these romantic slow chess moves, we will chronically run out of time and not attain either our creative or, relevant to this treatise, our competitive goal. This reveals the game of blitz to be not an elegant beast. Correct play advocates the barbaric over the beautiful in the aim to win the game, not create art. Only if we understand this will we be able to adequately benefit from blitz theory.

## *Time Victory Validity*

Many players feel that a victory gained on time during a resignable chess position is somehow of an inferior caliber than one resulting from brilliant over the board play. This idea is consummately illogical and must be discarded if we are to become competitive players. Persons who believe that the clock should only assist in speeding up a slow chess game to avoid boredom must directly be deemed *uncompetitive* contestants, since *the goal of the contest is to <u>win the game</u>*.

While the only way to win in slow chess is to checkmate our opponent, in blitz we can win either by checkmating him or by forcing his flag to fall. For example, if we just shuffle our rooks to and fro until our aggressor's time expires, we have absolutely attained our goal in a perfectly legitimate, honorable way, and deserve every bit of praise as one who wins through majestic strategic method. The additional time strategy for victory is precisely why the clock is on the table! When the victor accomplishes his task, it must conclude that he was the better player during the contest as only he succeeded in reaching his goal. If we ignore in the slightest the fully integral and consequential time crisis, then we simply do not appreciate the nature of the contest before us. If we win on time with an inferior board position, it is by no means conclusive evidence of poor chess strength, but rather can often be testament to prudent blitz strategy, for instead of depleting our time by solving the calculations, we may have realized the fertile chances of blitzing our opponent off the board. Perhaps we could have also out-played him over the board. *Any type of win manifests exactly a net adroitness of the victor, and a net shortcoming of the loser... no more, no less.*

## *The Digital Chronometer*

As will be manifest in the pages ahead, it is completely necessary for the competitive player to have available the <u>exact</u> time situation of the contest at any point in the game. If he doesn't, he will not be able to correctly implement his strategic arsenal, and much of his blitz skill will be rendered harmless.

To compete with maximum potential we must use a digital clock that clearly tells us, second to second, the time status of the game. The bottom line is that analog clocks simply do not permit a modern blitz arena, and must be discarded.

## *Know The Rules*

Are we good chessplayers if we aren't sure whether bishops move diagonally or flatly? Well then, how can we be good blitzplayers if we don't know all the rules of blitz? The fact is that most players don't know the rules, and get swindled as a result. It is essential to be certain of these standard rules of blitz chess as disputes frequently surface. The following is the official WBCA rules of blitz. Know them inside and out.

# World Blitz Chess Association Official Rules

*Approved by the advisory committee of Nick Defirmian, Max Dlugy, Yasser Seriwan, Ron Henley, Danny Kopec, Joel Benjamin, and Walter Browne.*

**1.** Each player must make all his moves in the five minutes allotted on his clock. This is the standard International Blitz time limit for all WBCA events. It is the only time limit which will be WBCA rated.

**2.** All the clocks must have a special device, usually called a "flag", marking the end of the time control period. Either player may object to using a computer clock provided they produce a clock with a standard face. In the event that both players prefer their own standard face clock, the player with black will have the choice each game.

**3.** Before play begins both players should inspect the position of the pieces and the setting of the clock, since once each side has made a move all claims are null and void.

**4.** Each player must push the clock with the same hand he uses to move his pieces. Exception: Only during castling may a player use both hands. When capturing, only one hand may be used. The first infraction will get a warning, the second a one minute penalty, and the third will result in the loss of the game.

**5.** The arbiter should state at the start of the event the direction the clocks are to face, and the player with the black pieces then decides which side he will play with that opponent.

**6.** Except for pushing the clock neither player should touch the clock except:

**a.** To straighten it.

**b.** If either player knocks over the clock, his opponent gets one minute added to his clock.

**c.** If your opponent's clock does not tick, you may punch his side down and repunch your side; however, if this procedure is unsatisfactory, please call for a director.

**d.** Each player must always be allowed to push the clock after his move is made. Also neither player should keep his hand on or hover over the clock.

**7.** Defining a win

A game is won by the player:

**a.** who has mated his opponent's king

**b.** whose opponent resigns

**c.** whose opponent's flag falls first, at any time before the game is otherwise ended, provided he points it out and neutralizes the clock while his own flag is still up and that he still has mating material.

**d.** who after an illegal move takes the king or stops the clock.

**e.** an illegal move doesn't negate a player's right to claim on time, provided he does so prior to his opponent's claim of illegal move. If the claims are simultaneous, the player who made an illegal move loses.

**7a.** Defining mating material

Either two minor pieces (except king versus king and two knights), a pawn, a rook, or a queen will be sufficient mating material. No trick mates are allowed which means a lone king or bishop is insufficient unless a forced win can be demonstrated within two minutes.

**8.** Defining a draw

**a.** A game is a draw if one of the kings is stalemated even if a fallen flag is claimed simultaneously.

**b.** A game is a draw by agreement only if the players make the agreement during the game.

**c.** A game is a draw if the flag of one player falls after the flag of the other player has already fallen, and a win has not been claimed unless either side mates before noticing both flags down.

**d.** To claim a draw by perpetual check, a *four* time repetition is necessary with the player counting 1,2,3,4 out loud so as to make it quite clear and easy for the arbiter to assist. Claimant should stop the clock after the forth repetition.

**e.** If both players each have just one identical piece, either may claim a draw by stopping the clock if neither side can show a forced win within two minutes.

**f.** A game is a draw if one player has insufficient mating material when his opponent's flag falls or makes an illegal move.

**g.** In king and bishop versus king and bishop of opposite colors, with only one pawn on the board, or in two versus one in a clearly blockaded position, a draw can be claimed by stopping the clocks and summoning an arbiter if necessary provided there is no forced win within two minutes.

**h.** King and rook pawn versus king can be claimed as a draw once the defender is on the rook file in front of the pawn. King and pawn versus king can be claimed as a draw once the defender is immediately on the square directly in front of the pawn as long as it's not on the seventh rank.

**i.** King and rook and rook pawn versus king and rook is a draw if the pawn is blockaded by the king and there is no immediate win.

## Miscellaneous

**9.** If a player accidentally displaces one or more pieces, he shall replace them on his own time. If it is necessary, his opponent may start his clock without making a move in order to make sure that the culprit uses his own time while replacing the pieces. If a player first touches one piece, then moves another; his opponent can restart the player's clock and make him move the piece first touched. Finally, it is unsportsmanly to knock over any pieces then punch the clock. For a first offense the player will get a warning (unless he causes his opponent's flag to fall, in which case the offended shall get one minute extra on his clock.): for a second offense a one minute add-on will be imposed; for a third he shall forfeit the game. Thereafter the arbiter may use other penalties or expel a player from the event for repeated offenses.

**10.** In case of a dispute either player may stop the clock while the arbiter is being summoned. In any unclear situation the arbiter will consider the testimony of both players and any reliable witness before rendering his decision, which in all cases will be final.

**11.** The arbiter shall not pick up the clock except in the case of a dispute when both players allow him to do so.

**12.** Spectators and players in another game are not to speak or otherwise interfere in the game at hand. If a spectator interferes in any way, such as by calling the attention to a flag fall or an illegal move, the arbiter may cancel the game and rule that a new game be played instead, and he may also expel the offending party from the playing room. The arbiter should also be silent about illegal moves or flag falls (unless there are sufficient arbiters and they have agreed with the players to call them before the event started) as this is entirely the responsibility of the players.

**13.** When a clearly drawn position is reached, either player may stop the clock and appeal to the arbiter for a draw.

**a.** If the arbiter allows a draw as in rule #8, the game is over.

**b.** If the appeal is rejected then a one minute penalty is imposed on the player who stopped the clock.

**14.** A player who has played an illegal move must retract it and make a legal move on his own time. If no legal move exists with that piece then he may make any legal move. Illegal moves unnoticed by both players cannot be corrected afterwards, nor can they become the basis for making a claim, although a piece once touched must be moved. An illegal move is completed when the player presses the clock, whereupon the opponent may claim a win provided he has mating material.

**15.** A legal move is completed when the hand leaves the piece.

**16.** Moving the king next to another king is illegal, however neither player can play king takes king! This cheap shot will not be tolerated! Stop the clock and claim a win because of an illegal move.

**17.** If a player promoted a pawn and leaves the pawn

on the board, the opponent only has the option of stopping the clock while a replacement piece is found up until the end of the game.

**18.** An arbiter may determine that a clock is defective and may change clocks at his discretion.

**19.** Before a tournament the organizers should post at least two copies of the complete blitz rules in the tournament area unless there are fewer than twenty-five players, in which case one list will suffice. Posting one hour before play is advisable.

**20.** If the king and queen are set up incorrectly then one may castle short on the queenside and long on the kingside! Once each side has made a move, incorrect setups stay unless both players agree to restart.

**21.** Excessive banging of the pieces or clock will not be tolerated!

**22.** Finally, in all WBCA tournaments the decision of the arbiter is final; however, for future consideration the WBCA will listen to any grievances or wrongdoings on the part of any arbiter or player.

# STRATEGY

## *The Clock Is A Piece*

The most important concept in blitz chess is that the clock is a blitz chess piece just like any other; and thus, we should make a strong effort to use it for attack. If we don't, our opponent will attack with it and ultimately mate us with it (force our flag to fall). This being the case, it is imperative that we move quickly enough to exert pressure on our opponent. What is quick? In a standard five minute game we must average *one move every five seconds*. With this pace, we are preserving our ability to conduct a campaign both thoughtful and lengthy; though most importantly, we are forcing our opponent to maintain our heightened pace or fall into serious time pressure.

As many of our moves will indeed be less accurate than with slow chess, it is imperative that we discipline ourselves from frustration. The reason why we often don't find the best move is directly because of the necessary competitive pace at which we are playing. This is not something to be remedied, but embraced, for the truth is that our game is stronger for the time pressure we exert on our opponent. He must, in turn, adjust his game to this clock attack or be defeated. Thus, by healthy clock aggression the inferior quality of the chess is outweighed by the superiority of the time pressure.

*If a move is not played within about five seconds, it is necessarily an exercise in bad technique, and thus a bad move.* This means that the best move on the board is only the best move in blitz if we find it within five seconds. With the exception of very complicated positions (which must be defined as rare) no move should exceed this limit. Perhaps a slower pace may produce more accurate moves; however, these better slow chess moves will never see their fruition as we will lose on the clock. The crowd may gasp at overlooked brilliancies, but such emotional discouragement has no basis as it ignores the fact that we are in a time crisis and are playing with optimal technique since we continue to execute effective moves within the critical five second interval.

Some hold the belief that they may correctly spend more time at the beginning of the game, as long as they speed up in the final minute. They argue that once they achieve a technically won position, the game will play itself, so the remaining moves will only require a couple seconds each. This is callow zeal. These persons will not have time to convert even a simple position, and will bungle it away. The weathered combatant knows the tenacity hidden in even the most basic positions, and therefore prepares himself to tiptoe through myriad swindles. It is not the exception but the rule that without appropriate time the leader will blunder.

It does not require extraordinary talent for the regular

blitz player to maintain this pace. Only simple mental effort is needed. If we assume a lethargic attitude at the table, then it will prove challenging; however, an honest decided effort will get us right up to speed. If we are unable to play a satisfactory game of chess within this pace, then we must practice if we hope for enduring success.

## *Eliminate The Ego*

If there is one thing for certain, it is that the average player's ego is thoroughly tied to the outcome of the game. After all, unlike most contests there is no luck in slow or blitz chess, so the total impact of a loss rests on the vanquished's shoulders. We can't blame the dog, the traffic, or the government when we're staring at our checkmated king. It's all our fault, and it does hurt.

In a game of logic and psychology there is no room for teeming emotions as they only cloud our thoughts, but with such a sting looming at the possibility of a defeat, only a conscientious player is able to play with his emotions at a minimum. This fact is wonderful for us because with some practice, we can greatly reduce our emotional affectation while our aggressor implodes inside his. *By simply releasing the excessive importance from the outcome, and appreciating the fact that our emotions do radically influence our play, our game will improve dramatically.*

The fact is that most players neglect this shortcoming. They devote five hours to investigating the most recent *Informant*, but can't find five minutes to investigate themselves. Perhaps it is too unpleasant. Perhaps most don't believe their emotional state to be relevant. Whatever the case, emotions run rampant in all chess competitions. Thus, the more one can extricate his ego from his play, the better a player he will be, and the greater will be his advantage over his opponent.

## *The Cardinal Rule*

Easily the most important habit we must practice is to *diffuse our opponent's superficial tactics as soon as possible.* This means releasing pins, moving pieces away from forking squares, sheltering our king from obvious checks, etc. Of course this is most often a good policy in slow chess also, (as many ideas are in this book) but while in slow chess it is correct to weigh the timing of our attack versus that of our opponent's, this is not the case in blitz chess, *for the time and effort required for such thought in a series of blitz games is far more valuable than the accuracy lost in our individual moves.* Consider the following position...

## Maroczy-Bogolyubov
## Dresden 1936

In a slow game, the correct move is 1.dc because black's bishop fork at c2 is off limits as white then plays 2.Rxd8+...Rxd8 3.Bxf7+ winning. If black chooses 1...Rxd1+ 2.Rxd1...Bxc, white can no longer immediately play 3.Bxf7+ soundly because of the cool ...Kf8 4.BxQ...BxQ; however, white has an offensive resource in the elegant 3.Qa2! Thus, after due calculation, he may soberly continue aggressive operations.

Now consider the same position in a blitz game. The time and mental strain required to calculate all this clearly and with confidence is far greater than one can afford. In a blitz situation the correct move is the wisely simple 1.Rbc1 because it diffuses the obvious fork and pin tactics threatened, thus holding our position with minimal time and strain lost.

In slow chess, the first priority in an open game is to castle. This is true tenfold in blitz, for not only will the ill placed king prove ripe for a variety of tactics, but also the accurate defense we will have to erect will surely cost a premium on the clock. Sometimes in slow chess we can calculate a Mikhail Tal battle plan in which the king commands his troops from the center of the battlefield. In blitz leave this only to Mikhail Tal himself! As soon as a center file breathes, we must get our king safe!

## Max Lange Attack

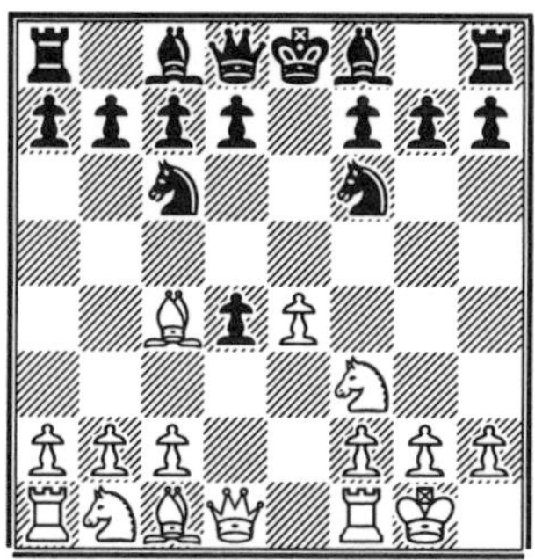

Neglecting to castle is not even worth a center pawn. In a slow game 5...Nxe is sound and strong as the ensuing aggression can ultimately be parried; however, if we are not already versed in this opening, are we really going to figure out the ensuing variations in five seconds?! Of course not. A good blitz player respects this fact and will respond with a humble move such as 5...d6 or at least 5...Bc5 with his eye on an expedient castling to safety.

A tactic that deserves specific comment is the back rank mate. As a rule, we create luft on the first hint of back rank weaknesses. Back rank threats, and actual mates account for an inexcusable amount of blitz losses. Perhaps the luft is not immediately necessary. Perhaps it is ugly, or creates weaknesses around the king. Perhaps we will lose the initiative. In blitz such excuses are irrelevant. Make luft or suffer the consequences!

## *Tactics: The Soul Of Blitz*

*The more our playing style embraces tactics, the stronger will be our blitz game.* This is true for two reasons. Firstly, individual positional gains are less destructive in themselves than are tactical blows-- It is easier to recover from a backward pawn or a bad bishop than from a royal fork. While it is rare that a player will hang a rudimentary tactic in a slow game, in blitz even the master routinely hangs pieces because the time crisis inevitably forces slip-ups. Thus, tactical aggression bears many more fruits than a positional siege because of the direct, conclusive consequences of a tactical oversight.

Secondly, it is possible to steer *all* situations away from positional channels to tactical skirmishes since closed positions can always be opened, piece play proves potent over pawn pushes, checkmate threats must forever be respected. In slow chess a positional player may successfully arrest these tactical maneuvers with the consequences of his prophylactic net. He dulls his opponent's tactical goals, and angles against weaknesses with individual moves not as important as their overall theoretical aims. Finally he immobilizes his opponent in static shortcomings. In blitz these shortcomings are far outweighed by the crushing force of the combination of the tactical savagery and the clock.

## Modern Defense

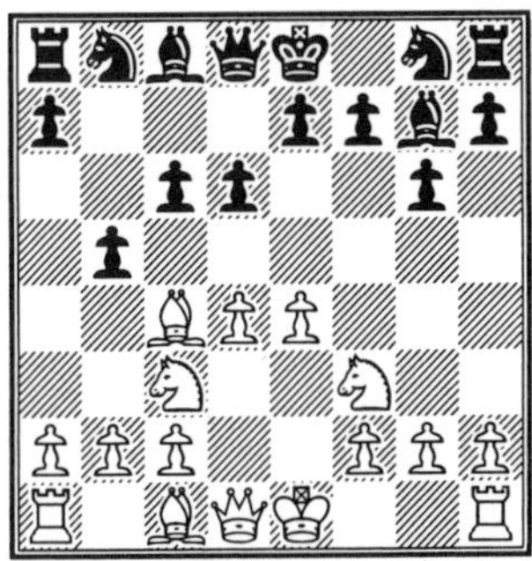

Here is an example of an attempt to enforce a positional campaign easily refuted by a tactical gauntlet. If white wishes, he may fire 6.Nxb5!?...d5! 7.Bb3...dxe4 8.Ng5 with a double-edged slugfest.

Other times the situation requires more of a positional concession, but once again, the resulting familiar tactical flavor combined with the time strain dominates the contest.

## Benjamin - Christansen
## 1997 US Championship

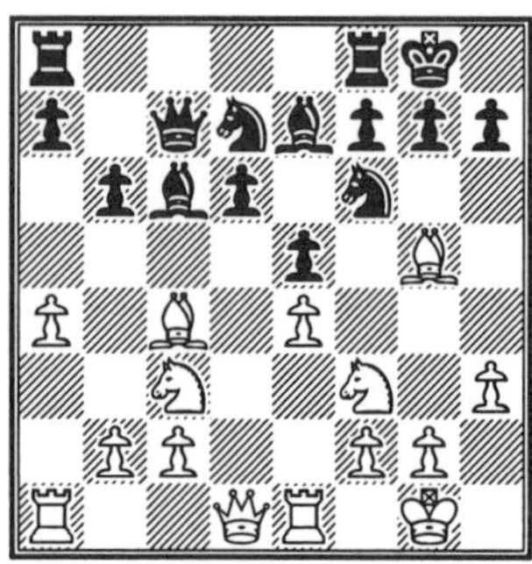

Here black made a brazen bid for chances by introducing tactics with the not quite sound 12...Bxe4 which gets into trouble after 13. Bxf7+, but he got away with it as white, under the blitz strain, only found 13.Rxe4. Black continued to liquidate his inferior position, and gained a satisfying draw. As we can see, even the world's best often cannot cash in on concessions yielded for tactical wrestings in blitz.

Because the time crisis forces mistakes, and because the tactician is so able to steer the game to conditions that prove the most ripe for these such mistakes (tactical conditions), *it follows that the victor will necessarily be the player who is most adept at thriving in these sharpest conditions.*

So then, our tactical acumen must be up to par. If it isn't, we must study and practice until it is. There are plenty of books out there filled with tactical quizzes and theory from which we can benefit. One must read them again and again until he feels comfortable enough in standard tactical encounters.

The following is a series of basic tactical exercises. If it proves too challenging, then our tactical skills need improvement. The solutions can be found at the back of the book.

*Tactical Exercises*

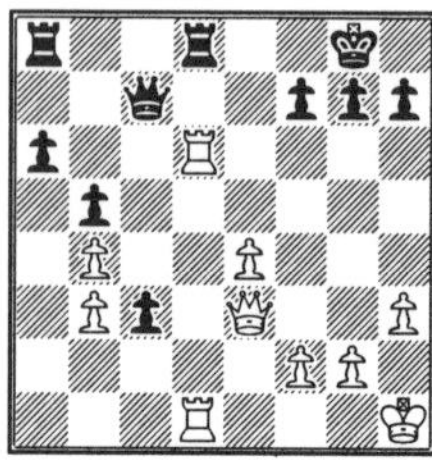

1.

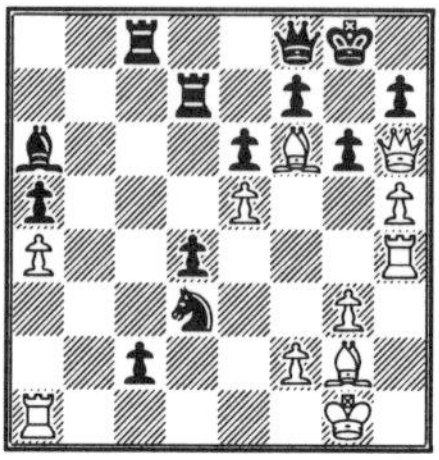

2.

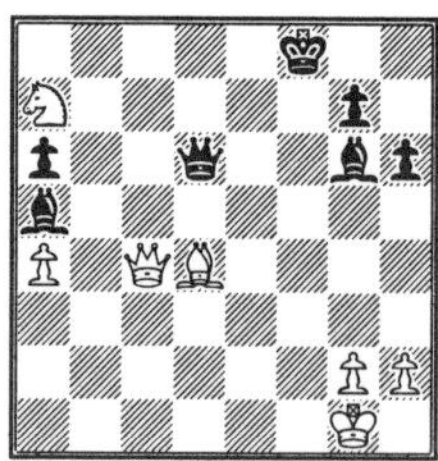

3.

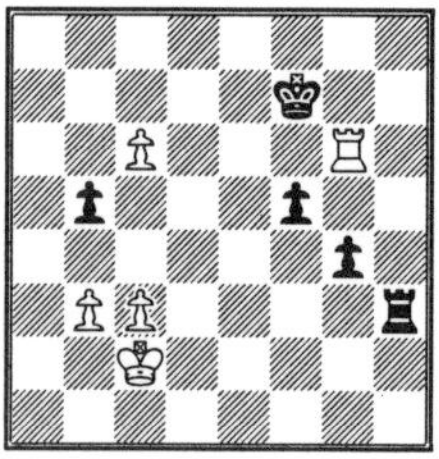

4.

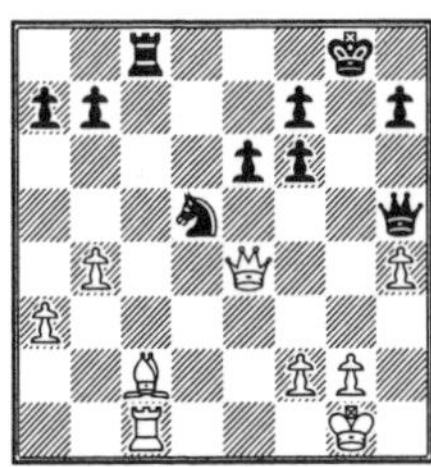

**5.**

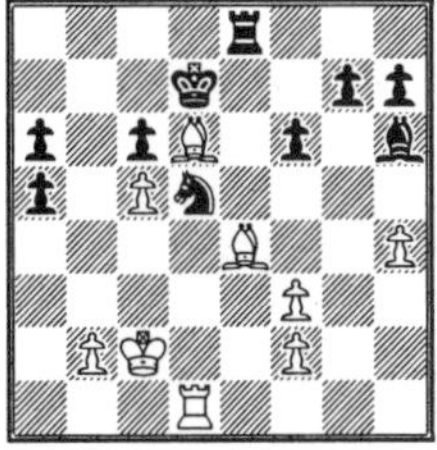

**6.**

**7.**

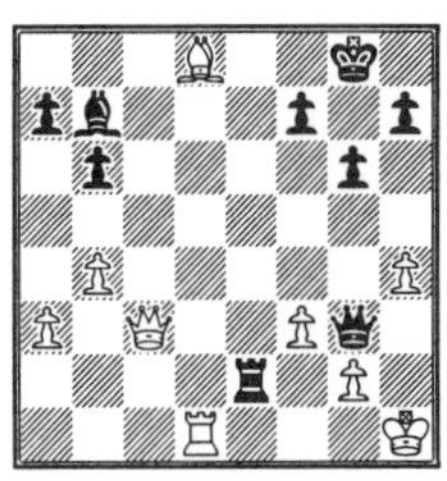

**8.**

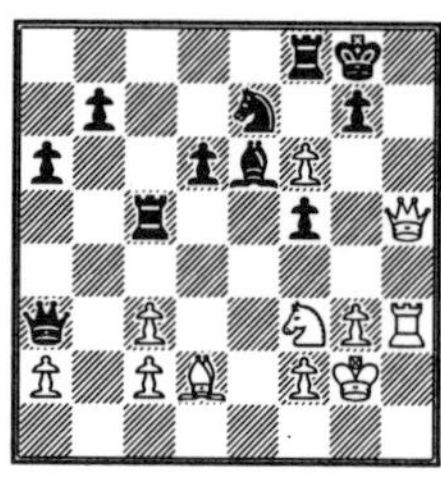

9.

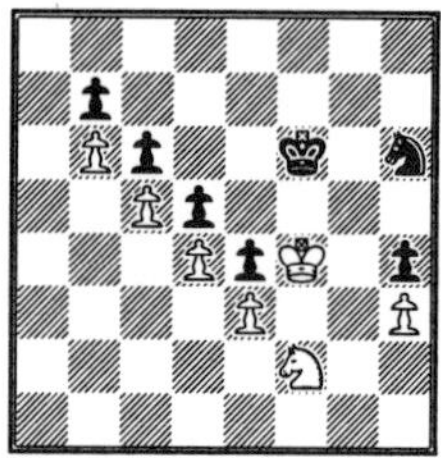

10.

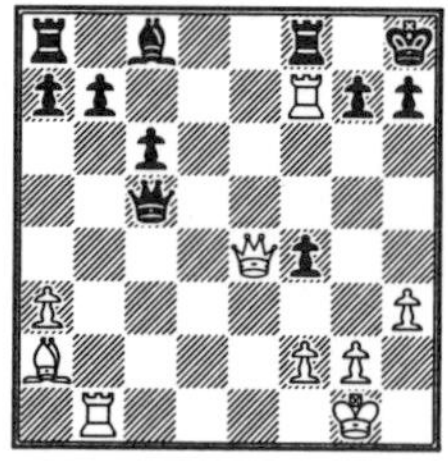

11.

12.

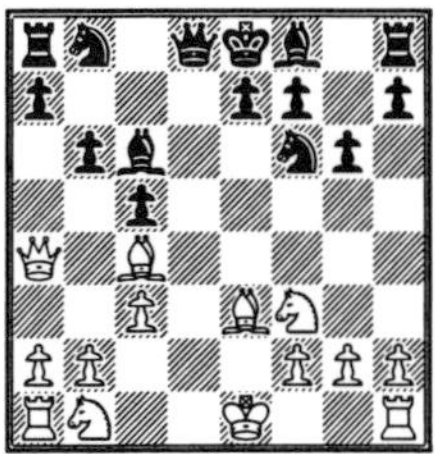

**13.**

**14.**

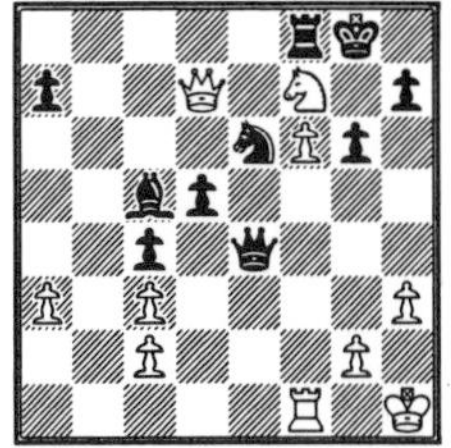

**15.**

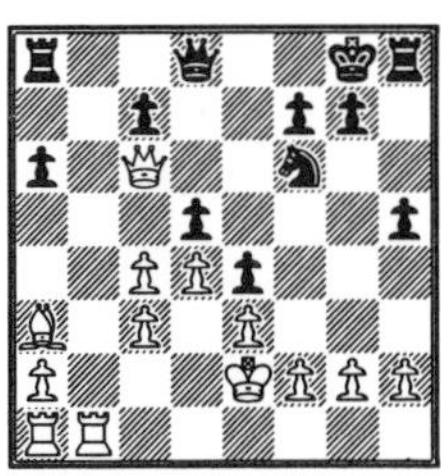

**16.**

## *The Best Defense Is A Good Offense*

This is true manifold in blitz chess because the consequences of a failed attack is a mere loss of initiative, while that of a failed defense is the loss of the game. Because of this fact the attacker has the luxury of being less accurate than the defender. *Since this accuracy is exactly the ingredient in dearth supply, an overwhelming advantage is gained simply by seizing the initiative.*

This being the case, it is best to adopt a campaign of heightened aggression. We make every effort to create threats to force our opponent into a defensive posture. When faced with a choice of a solid yet passive position, or a sharp and double-edged position, we play the latter as it keeps our opponent's stress level to a maximum, creating the most conducive environment for a decisive miscalculation.

## *If A Sacrifice Looks Good, Then It Is Good*

In slow chess an unsound sacrifice is ill-advised because it is too likely that the opponent will calmly calculate an adequate defense, and then convert his material advantage to a win. In blitz, however, he has not the time nor serenity to calculate such a defense, and will probably succumb to a flag fall or a blunder.

While the advantage gained from the opponent's lack of time to calculate the consequences of a sacrifice is obvious, the psychological advantage from his lack of serenity merits investigation. Anyone who has played even a little chess is acquainted with the sudden sinking feeling in his stomach when a knight or bishop comes crashing into his bulwark. He assumes we would never enthusiastically seek a permanent material deficit, and concludes that our attack must be irresistible. Such thinking has been reinforced for a chessplayer's entire career, so it is a safe bet that his immediate inclination will be to find our supposed winning line. If he finds none, his next resolution will be to decline the sacrifice as he will be convinced its solution is over his head.

## Tal - Hodgson
## 1974 Camndentown Simultaneous

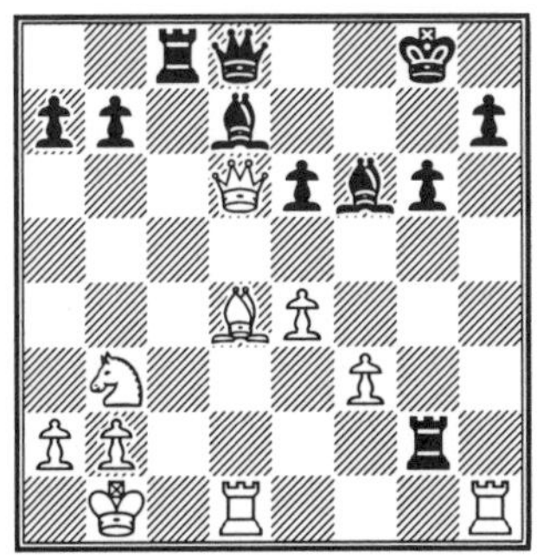

Here Tal speculatively played 1.Rxp, surely with the appreciation of its significant psychological consequences in addition to the tangible lines it opens. Even though simple analysis seems to reveal 1.Rxp to be a technical failure (1...KxR 2.BxB...QxB 3.Qxd7+...Kh6 4.Rh1+...Kg5 5.Qd2+...Qf4), Tal's opponent declined the material with 1...Rc6?? 2.QxB and quickly lost. He was defeated through psychology.

Even if our blitz opponent finally accepts the sacrifice, its destructive vibrations will be felt for the remainder of the contest. He will be focused only on defending for a good many moves to come, thereby extinguishing any healthy attacking aspirations he might have had. As there is always some level of intimidation instilled in an opponent when we play such a seemingly stellar, contemptuous move, his calculations will now be consummately confused by the anxiety from which he will no doubt be suffering.

All this ads up to not so much of a physical action on his position, but a psychological maelstrom that leaves him in emotional tatters. In some instances his play will drop a full class, and he will now take about twice as long to move. As a matter of fact, 80% of Mikhail Tal's successful slow chess sacrifices have been refuted in post mortem analysis, yet Tal was world champion. Thus, the success of the sacrificial strategy has been proven. If we simply follow up our blitz sacrifices with inspired fervor, there really will be no way he can win the contest.

Since this psychology behind a sacrifice is so potent, we may boldly yet soberly embark on a sacrifice based purely on a psychological platform. We do this by playing an outright bluff!

## Koblents - Tal
## Riga 1957

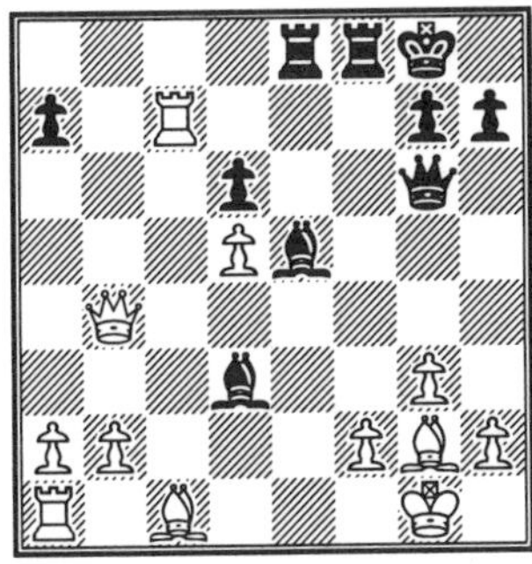

In the above, the slow chess move 20...Rxf2 is adolescent romance, but it is not hard to appreciate its convincing appearance. Even if we are sharp enough to realize that white can ultimately hold on to his material, it is sometimes recommended in blitz to proceed anyway with the aim of crushing our opponent under the involved psychological strain.

An additional reason advocating the occasional bluff is that when we do play a solid sacrifice, our now incredulous opponent is more apt to disbelieve us and take the bait. Now we may paint the board with our elegant combination amidst the oohs and aahs of the crowd. While slow chess rarely provides a credible opportunity for the dramatic sacrifice, there are more than enough chances in a session of blitz. This is our chance to really have fun!

Essentially, the bluff combined with the sound sacrifice forces our opponent to weigh every move individually, a consequence that is quite steep for an environment that already demands so much mental capacity. Because of this, even speculative sacrifices are often recommended. If the sacrifice looks sound enough, then these added elements will push the decision much past the affirmative.

# OPENINGS

Since a tactical initiative is so successful in blitz, the most effective opening repertoire is mercilessly aggressive. If our opponent isn't fluent with the positions, then these openings alone should provide us with enough pressure to win the games either on the board or the clock. If he isn't even familiar with the positions, the games will play themselves.

## *Essential Diversity*

As we play sessions of consecutive games versus the same opponent, we must not make it easy for him to learn from his mistakes from game to game. When we smash him with the same opening two or three times in a row, we must preserve this valuable weapon by playing something else for a while, and then something else again. Now he will always be on his heels. After a while we may return to our bread and butter, and let him fall for the exact trap that tripped him up just a few games ago!

Creating and maintaining this relentless atmosphere is as important as any aspect of our game. This being the case, it is essential that we acquire a broad opening repertoire.

## *White Openings*

For starters, I believe 1.e4 to be best in blitz. While many cases can be made for 1.d4 or other first moves in slow chess, one must remember that the savvy blitz player is pursuing inspired tactical territory. 1.d4, 1.c4, and 1.Nf3 are, of course, solid and dynamic; however, they lack the direct tactical nature of 1.e4. This is because after 1.e4, black must either accept tactical activity with 1...c5, 1...d5, or 1...e5, or be condemned to a drawn out uphill battle for equality. The positional alternatives for black's first move do him no good as they can be twisted to tactical channels through forced transposition. For example 1...Nf6, 2.Nc3...e5, 3.f4 twists the elusive Alekhine's Defense into the sharp Vienna Gambit.

If white doesn't seize the opportunity to move his king pawn out two squares at his first opportunity, then black can squelch its timely emergence with the simple and strong 1...Nf6 at which point the contest already begins a basically forced journey into a positional labyrinth. It is true that all games can assume a tactical flavor; however, *it is most easily achieved with the ever-sound 1.e4.* This being the case, it only makes sense to play accordingly.

The following is a sharp and varied opening repertoire. It should be noted that part of its success comes from the interrelatedness between many of the openings. The pawn structures, tactical motifs, and strategic aims often overlap between these setups, so the play of one reinforces another. While there are many aggressive and tactical lines one can employ, these are my suggestions...

## Against 1...e5

I promote the Italian bishop (3.Bc4) over it's Spanish counterpart (3.Bb5) for the direct pressure on black's Achilles' heel at f7. Perhaps the pin of the queen's knight has more substance in slow chess, but this is not the case in blitz.

### *1. The Evan's Gambit*

This is a gem for blitz play! For the expendable "b" pawn we gain a dominating, dynamic center, thorough activity, and a nasty attack on the king.

### *2. The Danish Gambit*

The rapid threats along the "e" file and on f7 combined with the raking bishops will ensure enough chances for at least a time win. We need not worry about the pawns as our opponent will never have the time to cash them in.

### *3. The Scotch Gambit*

Gary Kasparov employed the Scotch Game at the world championship level in slow chess. Enough said.

### *4. The Max Lange Attack*

Although perhaps superficial for a slow chess game, the beauty of this opening is that it is really one long series of memorized moves. Either our opponent knows the other side of it fifteen moves deep, or gets smashed before we even start thinking.

## Against 1...d5

### *1. "ed"*

The immediate opening of the "e" file combined with the probable harassment of the black queen provides fine initiative and tactics.

### *2. The Blackmar-Diemer Gambit*

The main advantage for our opponent in the Scandinavian (1..d5) lies in his familiarity of the ensuing positions. Therefore, simply take this familiarity back with a transposition, and gain a solid attack to boot.

A word of caution here is needed. It is of great importance that we avoid our opponent's tactics on the f1-a6 diagonal by moving our king to h1 at the first favorable opportunity.

# Against 1...c5

## *1. Any line with Morphy's 3.d4*

The Sicilian Defense is so tactical in its own right that not too much need be tailored from the main theoretical ideas.

## *2. The Yugoslav Attack*

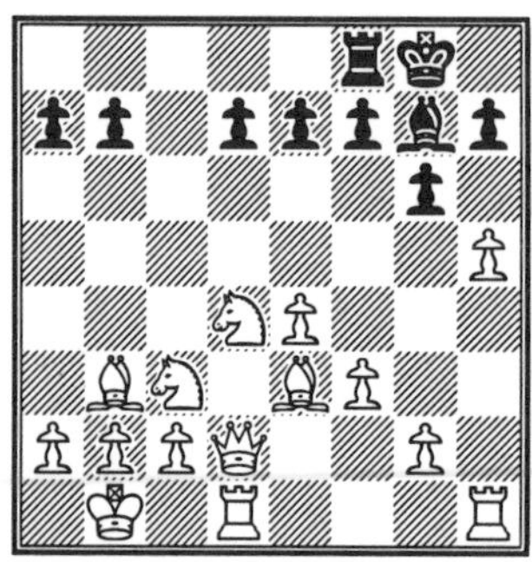

The magic in this attack lies in the perfect starting positions of the king rook and dark squared bishop. Since our opponent's fianchetto structure defines the weaknesses for us at f6, h6 and h7, we have a tailor made plan for a rapid and lethal battle. We just exchange dark bishops with our queen battery, then pry open the "h" file with our pawn.

## *3. The Smith-Morra Gambit*

By surrendering our "d" pawn, we gain the only central pawn at e4, a knight at its natural c3, the opening of both bishop diagonals, the d1-a4 diagonal for our queen, and the "c" and "d" files for our rooks. Meanwhile, our opponent has nothing anywhere at all, save the single a5-d8 diagonal, and a possible future backward pawn center. White's radically accelerated mobilization and unprejudiced dynamism combined with the retardation of black's campaign yields attacking potential of the highest order that can be gained from any opening gambit.

### *4. The Wing Gambit*

By relinquishing only the runt "b" pawn, we remove black's influence over d4, and gain a broad, sturdy, and mobile pawn center which cannot be ignored in an open game. In addition, our dark squared bishop may now pester at the a3 post. All in all, this is a very well motivated undertaking.

## Against 1...Nf6

## *1. The Vienna Gambit*

As previously mentioned, the main lines run into this gambit by 2.Nf3...e5, 3.f5

If black takes the pawn, 4.e5 will send the knight home for a browbeating. If he doesn't, then we can terrorize along the "f" file.

### *2. The Blackmar-Diemer Gambit*

(see above)

We can transpose to this if black chooses to play 2...d5

instead of e5.

### *3. Any tactical line after an alternative against 2.Nc3*

The best lines have been discussed. If black selects any alternative, he has accepted inequality, and we have accomplished our goal of an enduring initiative.

## Against 1...c6

### *1. The Advance Variation*

Significantly tactical and aggressive. While our opponent will no doubt be familiar with the first few moves, the lightning kingside activity and unstructured flavor will definitely knock him off balance.

### *2. The Panov-Botvinnic Attack*

The immediate and permanent open lines will grade against the calm and rigidity of the Caro-Kann player. As white's play is in the center, his initiative should endure his opponent's minority attack.

### *3. 4.Bd3 with a possible h3*

Tal's idea is all the more effective in blitz play. The Caro-Kann is essentially an attempt to institute the ideas of the

French Defense without the drawback of the bad bishop. With this in mind, white can derail the whole of black's aspirations by preventing the deployment of this bishop. After the exchange on d5, we simply do not allow the light squared bishop to develop by playing 4.Bd3. If he fights for g4's turf with an early Nf6, we quietly play h3 which decides the matter permanently.

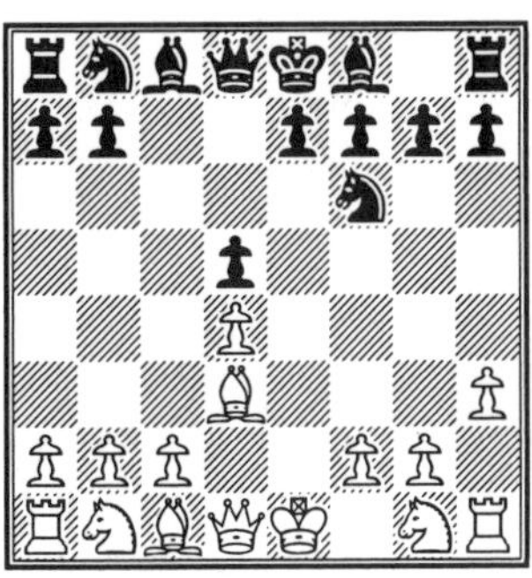

Black must either open up the position or accept the bad bishop. In either case, he has used at least thirty seconds in his decision, and will be uncomfortable in his setup.

## Against 1...d6

### *1. The Austrian Attack*

The rapid f4 is ideal to bully our opponent into immediate decisions. By rotating our spearhead between the pawn pushes f5, g5, and h5, we will have enough to keep him guessing. Experimentation with Bc4 as an alternative to Bd3 may bear fruit as well. Although black can try the recommended center fork trick with Nxe, the response Bxf7 is much more fierce in blitz conditions.

## Against 1...e6

### *1. The Milner-Barry Gambit*

As French players tend to expect a closed center, this gambit is wonderfully motivated as it violently disturbs blacks assumptions.

### *2. 3.ed...ed 4.c4*

While this does yield a basic equality, it is psychologically geared to strip black of his aspired positional expectations similar to our Panov-Botvinnik plans against the Caro-Kann. Since he hopes to spring his usual closed lines, we greet him with a hard-hitting open game in which tactical sparring will be the order of the day.

The potential of white's isolani should be appreciated as well. While its positional shortcomings often prove a nuisance in slow chess, its dynamic energy is far more effective in blitz.

## Against all others

If black embarks on any other plan of defense, it must be benign enough to condemn him to passivity with straightforward moves.

## *Black Openings*

Once again, the emphasis is on aggressive tactical winning chances, but now there is an added issue to consider: By having the luxury of the first move, white will have already given the game a flavor favorable to him. Because of this, we must make an even stronger effort to steer the game into channels both tactical and unfamiliar. In a slow contest it is usually prudent to stick with theoretically best lines, but in our blitz arena psychology plays too great a role to be ignored. Thus we will select our responses not so heavily based on slow theory, but largely aimed to rupture our opponent's psyche. Of course a theoretically poor opening is out of the question, but one that is psychologically as well as theoretically motivated takes precedence over another that is theoretically superior, but psychologically impotent.

# Against 1.e4

## *1. The Sicilian Lowenthal*

This is my first choice. Firstly, it perfectly caters to a hostile, combinative style. The direct seizing of the initiative and lead in development puts us in the driver's seat. Secondly, it is rarely seen in slow play so white will instantly be in deep and uncharted waters. I guarantee that 4...e5!? and the probable 8...Qg6, will together buy us at least forty seconds! The thematic attack on c2 is too stubborn to be remedied in five minutes.

## *2. The Sicilian Najdorf*

The most aggressive and studied line in slow play also pays off on the blitz board. No matter what white decides, we are ensured a fierce attack on the queen's wing. Although we aim to adopt openings unfamiliar to our opponent, this main line is so tactically sharp that it should be in every competitive player's repertoire.

## *3. The French Defense*

"Hold on there! I thought we were to play for open, tactical positions!" This is true. The reason why we make this exception is that The French is an opening that plays itself, and that means lightning clock strikes.

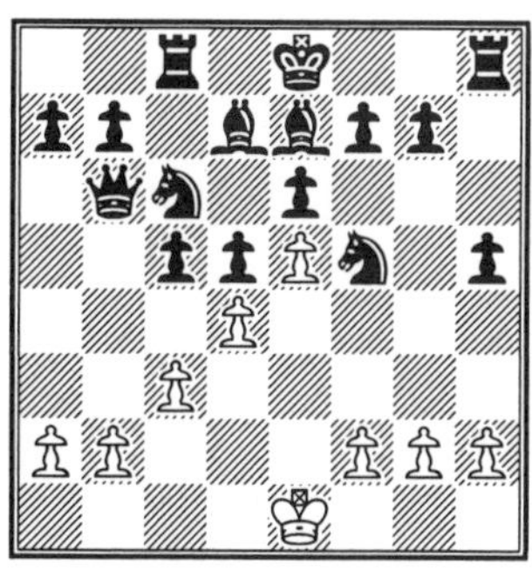

In most games, we play our pawns to e6, d5, c5, and h5, our knights to c6 and f5, our queen to b6, and our bishops on the central seventh squares. While white stumbles on his problems at d4 and b2, and ponders how to attack the rock in front of him in general, we may glibly paint our same picture time and again. It's as if our opponent is playing with a minute handicap. After play-testing it for years, I have conclusively found that only a small handful of players can smoothly handle this mischievous opening. Unless white has thoroughly studied his lines, black can at least play for time with superb results.

## Against 1.d4

Firstly, it should be stated that the foe in front of us is probably of a positional breed as he opts for the safe and sound queen's pawn thrust; therefore, we can immediately take solace in the fact that after we muscle the opening to familiar grounds, our tactical play will give us an advantage in the ensuing fight.

### *1. The Albin Countergambit*

A wonderful blitz enterprise. First, we can enjoy watching our opponent shift in his seat for ten seconds after 2...e5. Then commences the exciting setting of the many different traps depending on how white attempts to quiet our renegade "d" pawn. There is every chance he will be down material by move ten or mated by move twenty. If he isn't, his pawns will be doubled and isolated while his kingside remains critically unemployed and without promise. If he makes it to a middle game with a pulse, then he will only have about half his time left to undertake the daunting task of manifesting his unlikely tactical prowess. All this for a pawn!

### *2. The Benko Gambit*

This is sound and sharp in slow chess. By trading two flank pawns for white's “d” pawn, we remove his control of the prized real estate at e5 and c5, we gain immediate dominating pressure on the queen's wing with our heavy pieces, and a menacing bishop at a6. I really don't see how it's possible to not love this opening.

### *3. The Englund Gambit*

While I wouldn't advocate this in a six hour game, it fits blitz conditions like a glove. Firstly, it scores the maximum on surprise value as our adversary may never have seen the response 1...e5 in his life. Secondly, the anomalic queen and knight sorties on the queenside will hemorrhage seconds off his clock.

### *4. The Benoni Defense*

This is a perfect cap to our black arsenal against 1.d4. Tactical and uncompromising, it is a fine call to our job description. Upon seeing 2...c5, our opponent will no doubt begin to wonder what happened to his happier days of quiet maneuvering for modest holes and backward pawns.

### *5. Straightforward development against uninspired play*

If white decides to relinquish the advantage of his first move with something anemic such as 2.e3, or 2.g3, then we can consider our job done. Classical expansion will be sufficient for a good game.

## Against 1.f4

### *1. The From Gambit*

If he is going to voluntarily weaken his most vulnerable point in a five minute contest, then by all means punish him for it. He will be versed in this continuation, but the time pressure combined with the relentless pounding of "f2" must result in trying times for such an imprudent monarch. If he transposes to the King's gambit, 2...Bc5, or the Falkbeer Counter Gambit (2...d5) should teach him a lesson in blitz strategy. There need not be any further consideration for this opening, as he will admit his mistake by playing something else before long.

## Against 1.c4

### *1. Sicilian lines reversed*

While sound, c4 is innocuous in a blitz engagement. Play an immediate e5, engineer an early queen pawn thrust as in a Sicilian reversed, and we'll be off and running. White must be hoping for a positional game with such a commencement, so welcome him with the same blistering piece play as in the original tried and true white attack against such an idea. If he decides to surprise us with 2.d4, then 2...d5 introduces him to our Albin friend.

## Against all others

Spirited play and keen transposition will decide the day. We are equipped with enough opening ideas to menace any white beginning. Happy hunting!

# CLOCK PLAY

## *Pseudo Time Pressure*

Before we talk of specific clock situations, we must first discuss an unsound strategy commonly employed by the average player. When he gains a normal advantage in time, perhaps four minutes to three, he then attempts to convert his only slight advantage by fanatically blitzing his opponent off the board. This usually results in his blundering away the game. This unfortunate player put disproportionate pressure on himself to realize the conversion of his time advantage. In fact, he put himself in *pseudo time pressure.* Instead of calmly following his game plan, he acted as if he, not his opponent, was the one with the time problem.

Thus, in only the following circumstances should our game change from our usual five second pace. If we happen to have a standard lead on the clock, good for us. Our advantage is preserved in the disadvantage to our opponent, and our usual strategies are still best. If he is diligent enough to speed up to even again without faltering, then it is to his credit. Just don't believe that we should make an active effort to utilize his time deficit for it is not yet a weakness of enough merit to warrant a change in our strategy.

Now that we are leery of pseudo time pressure, we can discuss the instances in which the specific time conditions are of such significance that they alter the strategies of the board play.

## *Twice As Much Time As Our Opponent*

If our opponent has so critically fallen behind in time so that we have twice as much time as he, then we must adopt a new strategy to take maximum advantage of his negligence. In this situation our goal is to win on time, not on position, so unless we have an obvious board win, all of our actions will follow our time objective accordingly. We no longer care if he correctly solves the board combinations, for the board has now lost most of its consequence. *We have achieved a theoretical win on time of which its conversion is now only a matter of technique.* This is no longer fighting chess. If we play correctly, we will win.

If he hasn't yet realized the depth of the hole he has dug for himself, then we must do our utmost to keep him from noticing, and this may require a bit of acting. When examining the clock, our eyes shift without any head movement that might remove him from his distant thoughts. When moving the pieces and pressing the clock, *we must be as gentle and unassuming as possible.* We lull him into feeling there isn't any stress, or even another person across the table, just new positions for him to ponder. With a little luck, his competitive edge will float away. Now each captivated second carries him closer to defeat. Even if he notices his dire situation and begins to speed up, we maintain our tranquil conduct that reinforces his subconscious with the false sense of security.

We keep the pieces on the board, and the positions complicated. The pursuit of slight chess advantages such as doubled pawns, a better placed piece, or a queenside majority now takes a back seat to the prolonging of the positional tension which forces our opponent to spend time thinking. If he has fifty seconds or less, we should even forgo winning an exchange! Instead we play for mate and create tactical nuisances so that the board becomes an unrelenting minefield. Even if we're up material, we decline trades that yield simpler setups. We keep the contest murky and confusing. In effect, we are mating him with the clock.

## *Moving In Pairs*

Playing moves in couples of two may be the most effective clock strategy of all. To understand why, we must investigate the thought process of the blitzplayer. The natural way one plays blitz is to think basically one move ahead, as there is no time to analyze variations that one will never see. If a knight is attacked, the best blitz defense is usually the quickest, which in turn is usually the simplest. There may be many better "chess" moves involving double edged protection or counterattack, but the veteran player understands the prudent concession of precision for time, and executes the best blitz move he can find. Once he plays this move, he then commences to digest the new possibilities of the resulting position on our time. This being the case, we can see that the time he uses for analysis during our move is very important to him. *By removing this precious time for analysis from him, he will be forced to use more of his own time, thereby opening the fissure in his clock even wider. We remove this analysis time by thinking of our moves in pairs.*

While before we thought of the best move in about five seconds, we will now find the most probable two moves in about twelve seconds. We will play our first move, he will react as usual, but then we will play our next move immediately, thereby granting him no analysis time for the new position. *He is now forced to manipulate a completely fresh position on only his own time, a luxury he cannot afford.* The result will be either further time depletion, or the genesis of critical inaccuracies. Either way, he is doomed.

One might wonder where the advantage derives if he still has the same total amount of time for analysis in two moves. After all, even though he is given no time for the second analysis, he was given ten seconds before. Doesn't this extra previous time allow for the same analysis? No it doesn't. Even though he is given more analysis time initially, he cannot adequately apply these moments to his second move as the possibilities of what it will be are too numerous at the present point in the game. *Since the possibilities of plausible moves expands not arithmetically but geometrically, his task is simply too great.* This phenomena is best witnessed with a diagram and graph.

## Maxwell - Rudloff
## National Open, Las Vegas 1997

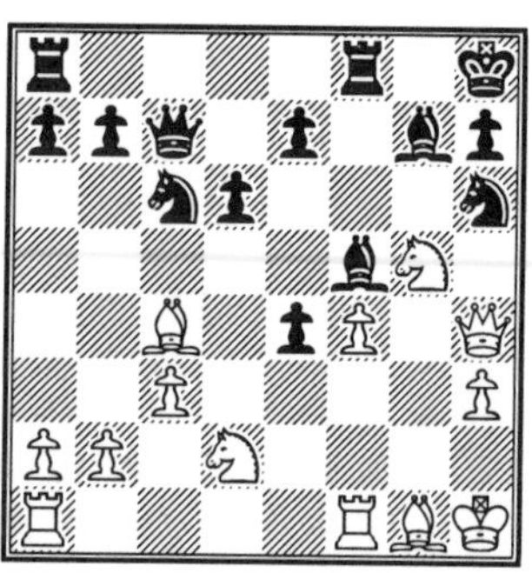

## *Maxwell-Rudloff*
## *National Open, Las Vegas 1997*

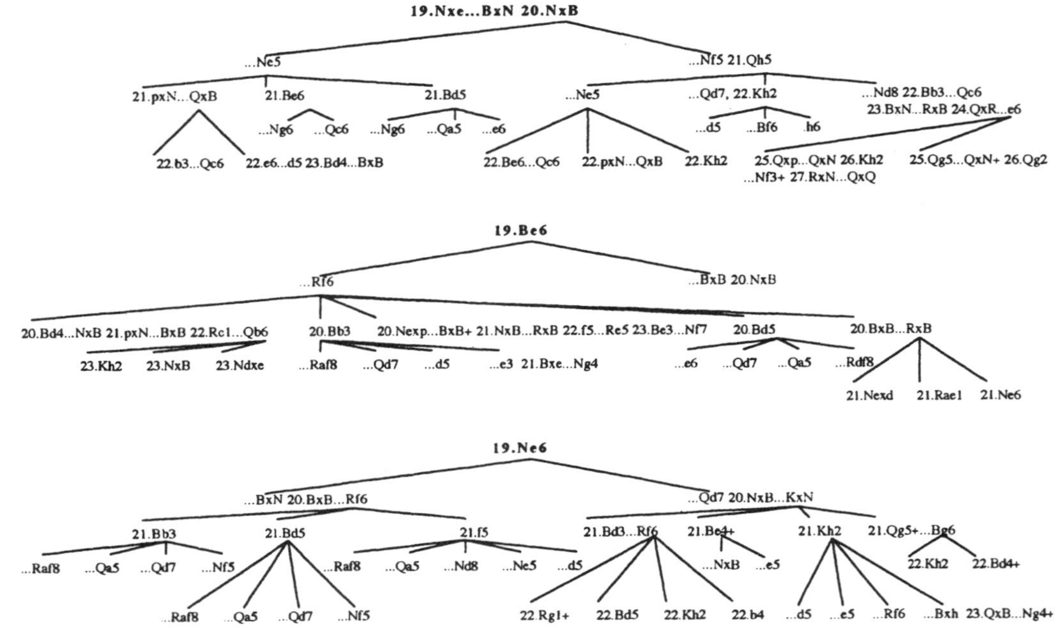

If his task is to see one branch into the future he will basically mull over the best responses to white's three probable candidate moves of 19.Nxe, 19.Be6, and 19.Ne6. As this is not that difficult, odds are he will find at least three of the six adequate responses satisfactorily (firstly either 20...Ne5 or 20...Nf5, secondly either 19...Rf6 or 19...BxB, and thirdly either 19...BxN or 19...Qd7.) If given the same amount of time on the following move, his task will be similar, and he will respond with the same level of accuracy. If we, however, give him more time on the first move, and then none on the second and expect him to play at the same level of accuracy, he will be required to analyze the total of *seventy eight* initial possible branches as opposed to the isolated fraction of the total he would have to deal with normally. His initial extra time clearly does not compensate.

This technique does cost us about a third more time overall than it costs him as we must now analyze geometrically added possibilities, *but our opponent has now given us this time to spare.* Unless we slip up, the game is ours.

## *Time Odds*

Time odds is the term given to the situation where one player starts with less time on his clock than his opponent, thereby granting his opponent an advantage.

The concept is rather straight-forward, and wouldn't be worth mentioning if it weren't for the significant psychological factor it adds to the challenge. When the average player is given an initial advantage in time, it is usually coupled with the backlash of feeling obligated to win. This added pressure to succeed goes mostly unrecognized, yet inflicts noteworthy damage to a player's ability that often outweighs his initial advantage.

This being the case, we can actually gain an advantage by first foregoing some time, so we should experiment with offering to handicap ourselves. A good start is to suggest dropping a minute off our clock granting our opponent a contest at five minutes to four. His advantage is significant, but not at all insurmountable as we will now play a second faster per move. At this point our opponent's ego eats him up. His determination to prove that he is at least equal to our caliber ruins him.

We can politely suggest this condition with something like, "Let me try five to four, just for fun." He wont want to give it to us as this would be admitting inferiority, but then we may continue, "Well, just prove me wrong. If it doesn't work out, we'll switch back to five-five." If he still doesn't want to comply, then we may nonchalantly suggest that he give us five to four if he wants. If he accepts, then we jump on it! We've just bought ourselves a free minute for nothing! *This trick doesn't work on us because we are informed blitzplayers who have learned the value of eliminating our egos!* We will not have the phantom pressure against us because we know the secret to the trick and will not succumb. It's still just a game with a goal that has now become easier. Either way, we come out on top.

If we begin to beat our opponent game after game with this handicap against us, his discouragement will become quite noticeable-- his head will shake amidst sighs and expletives, and his play will become reckless. Now it is time to go for the knockout. We politely suggest dropping to five, two and a half, "just to make things a little more fair." While he will quickly accept it because he starves for a win, his emotional stress will again multiply as the ego stakes have gone way up. While our task will be quite challenging as we only have half our time to make the same amount of moves, the massive pressure our opponent will feel from the deceiving time advantage will devour him.

To understand the theoretical as well as psychological origin of this deception we must delve into the actual nature of an advantage in time. When our original five minutes is handicapped, it seems to follow that our winning chances decrease proportionately. This is not the case because of the previously discussed nature of chess analysis. (see previous graph)

As we have investigated, our analysis does not run in an arithmetic progression, but a geometric progression. *Therefore, we will not be seeing less initial responses as before, we will only be seeing less deep, a restraint of far less consequence!* In other words, our critical immediate candidates will still remain intact as we can instantaneously find the few superficial responses to almost any move. In the aforementioned game, if we were forced to act immediately, we could confidently enough play 19.Nxe without analysis. We wouldn't be convinced that it was best, but it seems apparent that it is strong enough (it gains material, it centralizes, no pieces are hanging, etc.) Since it is the *breadth* as opposed to the surface of our thought that suffers, we can quite adequately operate under a time restraint.

Furthermore, much of chess analysis runs on abstract principles of attack and defense and piece activity. The average player will spot an open file or the need to activate a knight in a split second. Because these ideas are at the fore of one's thoughts, they remain quite intact during time deficits.

In addition, another very important detail must be appreciated. While it seems that we are playing with only half the time, we still have our opponent's five minutes with which to think. While it is not of the same quality as our time as we must think a half move ahead, it still is of great consequence to our overall allotted thinking time. *The truth is that we don't have only half as much time as before, we actually have 3/4 as much time.* The average player does not appreciate this.

Finally, while we still have all of our opponent's time, he now has lost half of our time! In reality both contestants will spend about seven and a half minutes on each game. The difference is that the quality of his time is a little better than ours. It appears that we are accepting a condition twice as difficult as he, when in reality it is far less.

When we consider these points, as well as the psychological grinder in which our opponent struggles, the mystery and magnitude of our advantage becomes obvious. What makes us better is our understanding and manipulation of the many different aspects of the contest before us. While he may convince himself that we're proving to be twice as good as he, our chess strength is about the same. *It is our blitz strength that is twice as strong!* He is playing slow chess at a fast pace. We are playing blitz chess at an efficient pace.

## *Play Under 15 Seconds*

When we have between fifteen and five seconds left, our time crisis has become so critical that it demands a new strategy. But first let's clear two things up.

This condition has no bearing on what our opponent's clock reads. The following strategy is structured purely to handle our specific situation, and will only be to our detriment if used at any other time. We will assume that our opponent has no more than a minute; for if he does, then we are simply too outmatched, and should move to the next game or opponent!

Secondly, time trouble does not necessarily mean that we have played inadequately over the course of the game. Many situations occur in which we play a fine, fast-paced game of blitz, and find ourselves with just seconds left. This is not any result of poor play; quite the contrary, it is often the result of blitz played at the highest level in which an epic battle brings both contestants to the brink of defeat! There is no reason to be embarrassed or afraid of this instance; instead, we can calmly and confidently apply the following technique.

When we have less than fifteen seconds, the importance of the board position greatly decreases as it will be irrelevant if our flag falls. Thus we no longer have the option of solving its complications as this requires time we do not have. How must we win then? Ironically our only option left is to use what is ailing us most: the clock. Even though we only have a few moments, it is much more plausible to now adopt an all-purpose plan for rapid movement than to attempt accurate analysis at an absurd pace. By energetically applying the following system, we find that we have much more than a mere glimmer of hope, for the following is a stubborn, resilient life support that will account for a remarkable amount of our victories.

### 1. The One Second Rule

As with our five second rule, it is of utmost importance that we adhere to this new tempo, lest we fall victim to inexcusable defeats. *We must now move at a rate of nothing more than one second per move. No excuses!* It will prove extremely difficult to perform with any chess accuracy, and blunders will occur, but any slower rate will completely extinguish our chances. Even though it may feel foolish to execute moves without analysis, it is the correct strategy demanded by the situation, and we must get used to it if we hope to improve.

## 2. Safety Mate Threats

As a checkmate by our opponent is still of the greatest consequence, it is vital that we extinguish such possibilities. Whereas before we might have had the allowance of walking a tightrope with our attacking and defending allotments, now the safety of our monarch is all important. We must identify tangible mating combinations and take immediate defensive action as there will be no time for analysis once they are put in motion.

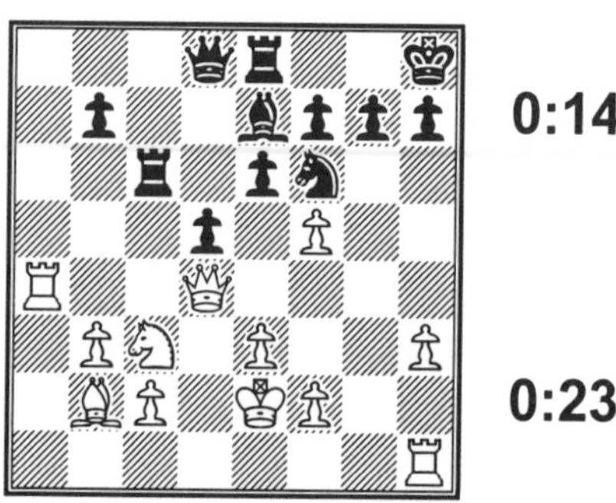


In the above example white has mating pressure on g7. Since this is not abstract hostility but a specific threat, black must respect it by defending immediately with something like 1...Bf8 so that he may not let it trip him up in the upcoming time scramble.

## 3. Disregard Basic Material Considerations

This means the loss of pawns and exchanges are now irrelevant, while the full loss of pieces are only of little consequence. We must believe this or lose on time! It may take a while for our conscience to let our pieces hang in the wind, but these are now skilled positional sacrifices! Of course we shouldn't simply throw away all the plastic we can, but we absolutely must move in a second. If our king's welfare needs the moment of consideration, then we must give his subjects zero.

## 4. Maintain The Tension

This is the heart of our strategy. We create and maintain conditions conducive to maximum time consumption by our opponent. In other words, we will give him as much to think about as possible so he strays from his vital speed play, and loses on time. We do this by keeping the board complicated and full of tension.

Although the maintenance of an involved position is the basis of a winning strategy in such situations, it is remarkable how most players strive for the exact opposite. They assume that since they now have so little time to think, they should give themselves the smallest possibility for error, and therefore either conclusively force the issue or humbly retreat. While this thinking is instinctive, it must be discarded for this plan yields no basis for success. How do these people expect to win? Why execute an attack or defense that will never see a fruition? If our opponent is not in time trouble, then we have just solved all his problems. If he does have a mutual clock dilemma, then we have mitigated all his mental pressure with our untangling of the position. In the end, a simplifying strategy is geared to help our opponent win!

Instead we make every effort to burden him with decisions. The desire to find the best chess move is seductive indeed, and often occupies even the wisest contestant, let alone the uninformed player. As this is the case, we offer our opponent an array of choices at every turn, and watch his precious seconds drip away as a result.

When we are on the defense, we no longer attempt to remedy insipid combinations as this discourages his attacking interest and thereby alleviates his detrimental mental involvement in the position. We have already looked to our king's safety by eliminating any mate threats. If there exists a way to grant him further security, it should *not* be achieved in this instance.

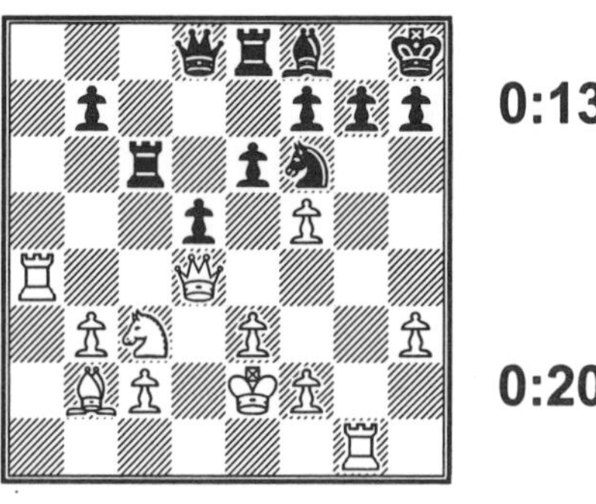

Here is a continuation of the previous position. Since there is no longer any real threat at g7, we can let our opponent consume himself in his aggressive ideas. We mustn't play something from slow chess such as 1...e5, but rather an indirect waiting move like 1...Qe7 or 1...Rc7 is recommended.

When attacking, only certain mating combinations should be executed. If we're not sure of the outcome of a series of moves, then this is the last time to play them. Their apparent threat works wonderfully for us, and must be preserved accordingly.

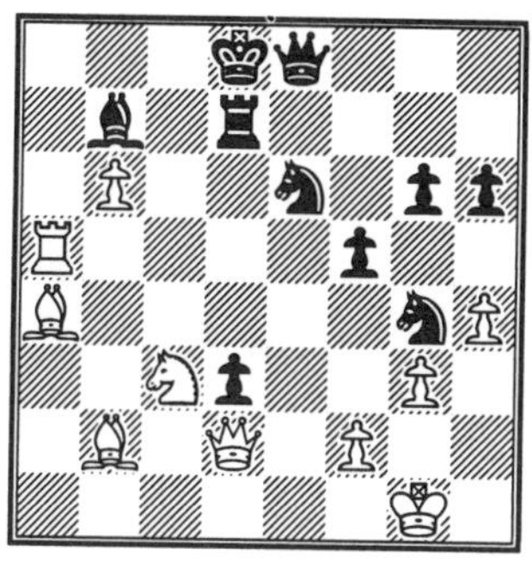

0:14

0:12

In this instance white has a fine attack indeed, but now that he is in a time scramble adequate analysis is not possible. As stated earlier, the easiest (and thus quickest) move anyone can make is a response to a superficial direct threat, so a reflexive move such as 1.BxR is an example of poor technique as it forces black into playing quickly (and thus correctly). The moves 1.Ra7, 1.Ba3, 1.Nd1, and 1.Kf1, on the other hand are all *equally best* because they succeed in the only immediately relevant goal of maintaining an involved position.

If the board at present is simple, then we must play moves without direct responses since these moves elicit the most curiosity, thus squeezing the most seconds from our foe.

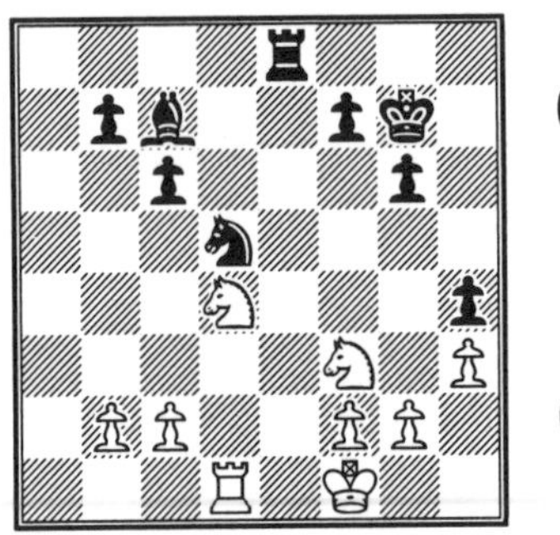

0:27

0:12

To keep our opponent occupied we need to do more than play a petty pawn prod such as 1.c4, since he will immediately see the reason behind our play, and quickly remedy it. If we abstractly maneuver instead, he will waste precious seconds struggling to find the relevance of our irrelevant actions. Decentralizing minor pieces (1.Nd2) and switching rooks to new files (1.Ra1) are examples that fit the bill.

## *Play Under 5 Seconds*

When our clock has just five ticks to expiration, the

time crisis reaches its zenith, and we must give it our full attention. We have done our best through the last ten seconds, but it has not been enough, and now we must change our strategy even further for this final phase of the game.

Firstly, our strategy remains to best him on time. Only staving off our eminent clock defeat matters, so material considerations are now completely irrelevant. While before we treated the chess play with a certain consideration, at this point we must totally disregard it as it no longer has any meaning. Now the best move is purely the fastest move. If our queen hangs, fine. Let's hope our opponent takes sweet time yanking it off the board.

## 1. The Split Second Rule

We must now move within fractions of a second, with the absolute maximum of a one second lapse. This is not impossible as in practice we often begin moving our piece just before the opponent presses his clock. *Whatever we do, we must not fall into the trap of pondering the position!* Years of reinforcement will no doubt interfere with our resolve to knowingly let pieces hang in the wind, but we must not waver. We just see that our king is not in check, then move!

We are simply looking for the fastest move possible, and this will be the first legal move found with the piece physically closest to the clock.

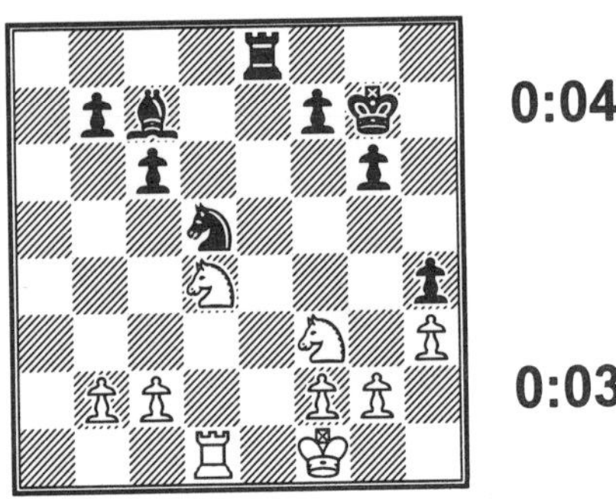


When fractions of a second count, the difference between reaching inches away and across the whole board is significant. We find the nearest piece, and just move it back and fourth as quickly as we can. In the above either 1.Kg1, 1.Nxh, or 1.g3 are all correct. We will not worry about the four move repetition draw, as it is only a factor if he calls the sequence out loud. Even if he does, we simply move to a new square on the fourth repetition. In this way it is possible to play four or five moves in one second!

## 2. Flag Scrutiny

We must pay close attention to our opponent's flag, and be sure to stop the clock at the exact instant it falls. Such scrutiny is all important as it is often the case that our opponent's flag drops when we have a scant one or fraction of a second remaining. If we fail to halt our time at the precise point of victory, our win will turn into a lackluster draw. It should be noted that this split second stopping of the clock requires swift and accurate arm movement. It is strange that a bit of athletic skill is necessary in playing any sort of chess; nevertheless, it is the case here, and it will be responsible for many of our victories.

## 3. Falling Pieces

During these shoot-outs it is very common for a contestant to knock a piece over and fail to right it before hitting the clock. This is a violation discussed in rule #9 and may be punished by the immediate hitting back of the clock with the demand that the guilty party correct the position on his own time. Since this violation occurs so frequently, our active declaration of it is invaluable as the mere second in the balance can be all the difference between victory and defeat.

When we knock over a piece, we will attempt to slip by the violation by first hitting the clock and righting the piece on our opponent's time. If he moves before we can fix it, then we will move again, and once more try to right the piece on his time. If our opponent declares our violation, we are forced to correct the position accordingly, but this rarely happens as most players become too lost in the scrambling to remember to declare this violation.

## 4. Stripping Mating Material

One specific five second scenario must be dealt with differently. If we have a preponderance in material, but the probability of our flag dropping is too great, we must aim to benefit from the insufficient mating material condition noted in the rule "8f" by making every effort to snatch up our adversary's remaining pieces and pawns leaving his king alone, or only assisted by an ineffectual minor piece.

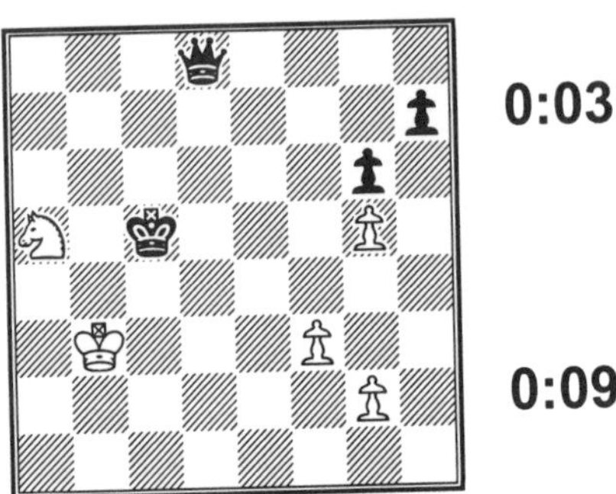


In this example the correct play is 1...Qxg followed by the capture of the remaining pawns. Now even if our clock reads zero, we will sustain not a loss but a draw as our opponent's army has not the ability to force mate.

# ADVANCED TECHNIQUES

By now we have a thorough knowledge of the skills needed to be a champion blitz player. If we stopped reading here, we would be quite ready to embark on a successful blitz career. There are, however, many clever tricks of the trade that can turn the tables on even the most hopeless games. The following section discusses such swindles.

It must be noted that if these techniques are given more emphasis than they deserve, they will hinder rather then help our game since even the most effective of these tricks pales in comparison to the importance of fundamental blitz play.

As in most disciplines, seemingly risky or contradictory strategy is often required to attain the greatest possible edge. While a lawyer attempts to gain the best outcome for his client, he will sometimes request that the maximum penalty be the consequence of a guilty verdict. While a doctor toils for the greatest well-being of a patient, at times he must subject him to deadly radiation and chemotherapy. Though we are discussing a mere recreational game, the same paradoxical nature exists, and should be appreciated accordingly.

As these strategies rely greatly on the unsuspecting

mind-set of the opponent, they must not be employed too often or our opponent will catch on to our antics and backfire them in our face. If instead we covet them as valuable aces in the hole by reserving them for only important occasions, they will yield much success and amusement.

## *The "??!" Move*

There will always be games that have gone too drastically wrong for any stellar combination or lightning play to remedy. In these instances it does not pay to expend valuable effort in the hope that our opponent will play some fantastic series of blunders that once again will grant us competitive chances. Instead the most prudent course is to take a conclusive calculated risk. If it fails, we may resign with a clear conscience, but if it succeeds, victory will be ours. As the game was worth almost nothing the move before, the risk taken to gain the win is easily warranted.

If the game is so severely lacking of a winning chance, we have no choice but to create one from nothing. This means that we must play a move that is totally unsound, but will turn the tables if overlooked.

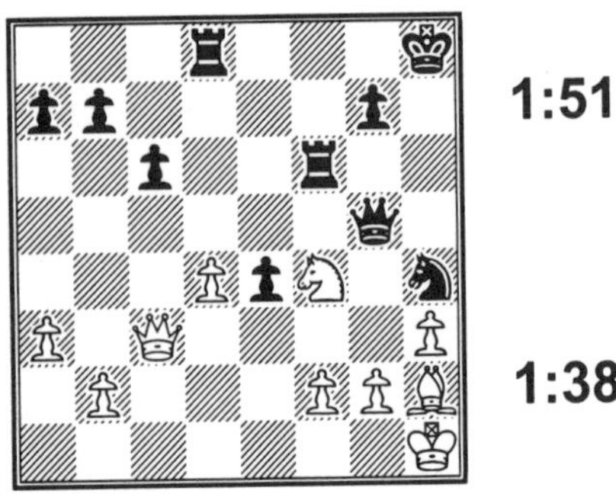


The white side is down two pieces and a pawn, and absorbing a savage attack to boot. As black's time condition is comfortable as well, there is no plausible long term strategy that will work here; therefore, we must find some move that, no matter how "chess" absurd, will give us a shot at victory. The suicidal Qa5+??! is now the order of the day. In most cases our adversary will snatch our queen hanging in the wind, but on a surprisingly good many occasions, he will overlook the obvious and hang his queen in turn! We may then deliver our blitz bolt from the blue and listen to the vociferations of our newly vanquished foe.

This ploy works often enough because of the favorable psychology at work in such a situation. Black is quite off guard. He is up a wealth of material, his position is crushing, and his time is far from concerning. This being the case, any move of ours must prove harmless, so he falls into the trap of giving our moves little heed. He will find the first plausible aim to our actions, and dismiss it accordingly. In the preceding case, the unassuming glance will resolve that white's motivation was a desperate hope to win the d8 rook. "After all, what else can he do?" he will think, at which point there will be seemingly no need for further consideration. He will play something like R8f8 and we will scoop the black queen and enjoy a victory from the jaws of defeat.

An effective "??!" move must be creative and subtle. As discussed, this ploy works because we dupe our opponent into thinking we are harmless, but this can't be done without some effort. No matter how strong is his position, a player will always take a moment to reason the motive behind our actions. Therefore we must provide him with a plausible one or he will not be duped. In the above example, if we move our queen to g3 then of course he won't play R8f8 for the danger to him is blatant. A better but still unsatisfactory try would be to move our queen to c5. While this is more subtle, it's chances of succeeding are slim as we haven't given him a motive as to why we would move there. With Qa5 we sell our opponent on our motivation to win the rook. This makes sense to him, and he may now easily overlook our real lethal intentions. Only with such care for artistry will this tactic pay dividends.

## *The Sloppy Piece Placement*

Like anything dealt with on a regular basis, the chessboard soon gains a unique familiarity with its player. It is no longer a block of squares on which sits a curious placement of pieces. Instead, it becomes an intimate, forever returning arena for the analysis of ideas. This awareness brings with it an expectancy of consistency for its exterior characteristics. We expect the squares to be essentially white and black, the bishops to be taller than the knights, the pawns to all look the same, etc. A good testament to this is when during a particular tournament Bobby Fischer petitioned the administration to find him a set in which the king could be better distinguished as the current one didn't have the characteristic Christian symbol atop its base.

Along with these expectations is the assumption that the pieces will rest in the center of their posts, and when one is placed with too much inaccuracy, the veteran player is greatly distracted at this "smudge" on the board. *By purposely creating such smudges, we can favorably distract our opponent into serious blunders.* Let's look at an example...

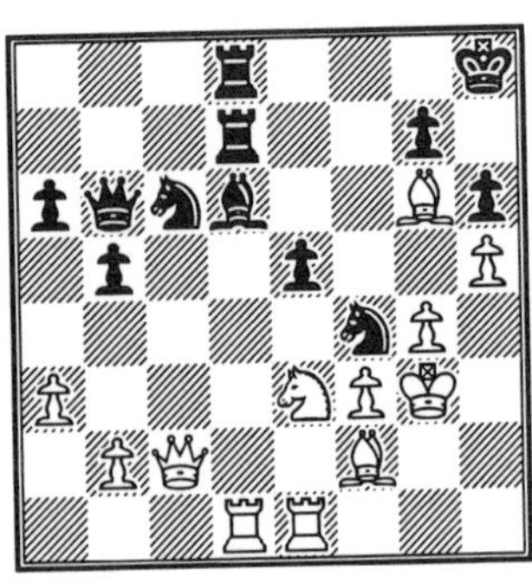

The move Nf5 creates a standard discovered attack on

the queen, and will be seen in a typical situation. By placing the knight not directly in the center of the square, but a good ways past the edge of the square, there is a fine chance that the opponent's flow of concentration will be jostled, and his view of the position will now be skewed in the direction of the "sloppy knight." Now that he is distracted to the wrong side of the board, there is every likelihood he will miss the attack on his queen, and leave it vulnerable to the naughty bishop.

## *Gift Time*

In many instances our opponent's clock ticks away without his knowledge. This can happen for a variety of reasons. Perhaps he has failed to fully push down the lever, maybe he was distracted when we made our move. It is often the case that he is so wrapped up in the position that he forgets the clock exists. Whatever the case, an instance like this is a valuable gift and should be coveted as such.

When it is noticed, care must be taken to hide any enthusiasm gained from the situation. We must remain still, as if engaged in thought. Although the situation proves very amusing, we must maintain composure by using the time to ponder the position, or we will fail to reap our full benefit.

If our opponent still hasn't noticed after thirty seconds or so, his suspicion will rise as to why we are taking so long. We now sell him further on our apparent meditation. While not over-doing it, a common clicked tongue and furrowed brow can buy twenty more seconds. By now he will be very puzzled by our failure to move, and most definitely discover his dupe. If he doesn't, we can sell him even further with an agitated shift in our chair. After this it is best to just sit still. Remember that in this acting, less is more.

## *Advanced Techniques Under 15 Seconds*

### 1. The Stunning Queen Sacrifice

While the unhurried opponent will spend due time if a position seems uncommonly crucial, he will not evaluate much of anything if he is in dire time straits. For him to now ponder consequences, they will have to seem decisive. Such a tall order can be found in a sacrifice of dramatic proportions.

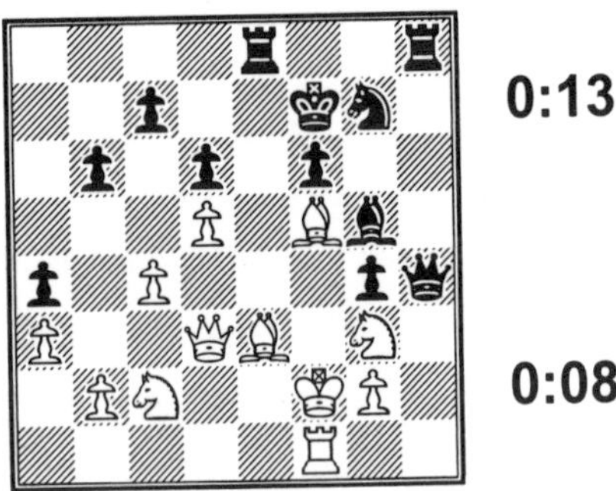


As stated in the fundamentals, material considerations have

very little relevance at this point, but the average player does not adequately appreciate this and can suffer as a result. We play a bold sacrifice with our "heaviest" piece possible, in this case ...QxN+, and loudly slam it down into the board while voicing some confident expression such as, "Wow is that beautiful!" or "Smash!" All this paints a very intimidating picture as it seems we have just delivered a magnificent death blow. With any luck, our opponent will now waste enough vital seconds to bring home a time victory for us. As his clock condition should be somewhat similar to ours, three or four seconds will be all we need to push him over the edge, and even a bargain at the price of a queen.

## 2. The Pseudo Check

In the great majority of blitz scrambles the average player seeks as many checks as he can against his opponent's king, no doubt taking refuge in the idea that as long as his opponent is in check, his position will remain safe. Because of this, all blitzplayers grow to expect a wild series of checks against them if they relinquish the initiative in such a scramble. Since this expectation is so firmly ingrained in the psyche, we can utilize it.

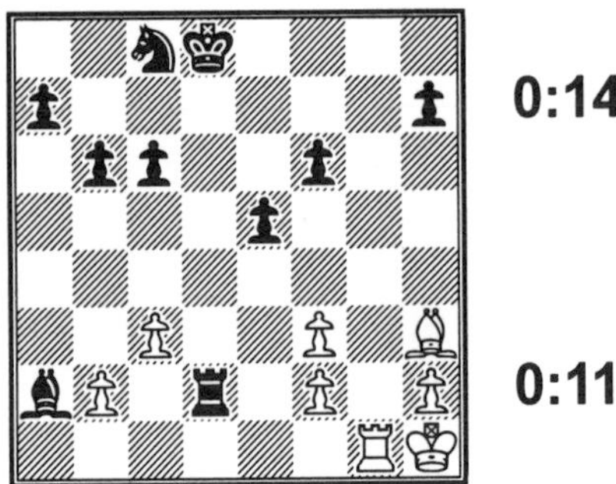


When we have an obvious check with a rook or queen, we don't play the check, but instead say "check" while merely cutting the king by placing the piece on the line adjacent to the check. In the above diagram, our opponent will expect the move to be the Rg8 check. Instead, we say "check" while playing the wily Rg7 blitz tactic! Now there is every chance that upon seeing the typical rook thrust he will move out of the anticipated check, and walk right in to our true check. We can then claim his illegal move as our victory.

This is a perfectly legal tactic. While the unfortunate mark may complain about the validity of the swindle, the fact is that there is no such thing as a "false check call." Vocal declarations of check have no relevance in blitz or slow chess. Only the board speaks of the king's danger.

# MISCELLANEOUS

## *Sportsmanship*

First and foremost, I'm an adamant follower of honorable conduct. If I feel something to be morally incorrect I will not tolerate myself to do it no matter how easily I may get away with it; and thus, I hope to influence the reader accordingly. For example, it is immoral to knock over a piece, purposely set it on a different square, then argue that it is correctly placed.

On the other hand, if I feel that an advantage is indeed within the arena of fair play even if it is somewhat devious, then I will ardently strive for its attainment. *Although the effective manipulation of blitz conditions may elicit ill feelings from its target, it is in no way illegitimate or unsportsmanlike.* We are in a fast paced, pressured arena. The legal utilization of these radical conditions is only prudent strategy.

As previously stated, both players aim to win using any means allowed them by the stated rules. Any player falling victim to a clever trick could have fairly employed the same trick on his aggressor. If the method is not of some cultural vogue, then so be it. Is it wrong in slow chess to hide a bishop on the corner of the board if it aims to deliver a sudden mate? Would it be more proper to tap our opponent on the shoulder and educate him of the impending hostilities? Of course not. Only a frustrated victim's ill-conceived ridicule is deserving of reproach since he is attempting to place blame on actions that satisfy all technical stipulations.

## *The Blade Must Be Sharp!*

In order for a weapon to be effective, it must remain finely tuned. Since the blitzplayer's weapon is his mind, he must take care of it if he aims to succeed. This means a healthy diet, adequate rest and exercise, and perhaps some form of vitamin boost before combat.

Many believe that intelligence is a permanent genetic function fixed at birth, so their physical health has no relevance to the quality of their calculations. This couldn't be farther from the truth. While I can site my own experiences with optimum versus poor health, the best advice I can offer is to experiment yourself. Eat fast food for a couple days, burn yourself out at the office, catch only a few hours of sleep, then play a session of blitz. In the following week take fine care of yourself and play again. The verdict will manifest itself.

Downing a large health drink twenty minutes before competing is an excellent habit for success. Carrot juice has been best for me. Vegetable juice is great. Protein smoothies work well. Now that our mind is fresh and fueled, we may slice through our opponents with razor sharp technique!

## *Trash Talking*

Many prefer to keep a cordial tone to the contest. During the session not much is said save an occasional remark of a sincere and respectful quality. Then there are others who prefer a politically incorrect competition. Now away from their professional world, they enjoy allowing the children within them to frolic in unrestrained, uncensored censure. As neither party takes the other seriously, spirited vocal exchange can prove both refreshing and comical. While contributing this delightful fraternity to the meeting, such banter also yields an added level of competition in which the better talker succeeds in decisively distracting and intimidating his opponent. This advantage proves significant enough to merit substantial effort for its acquisition. Put most simply, *the good blitz player knows how to talk trash!*

While it might prove humorous, there is no need to give examples of effective invective as we all can remember our days on the school playground. It is important, though, to prepare ourselves against the debilitating effect of such a barrage of insults. If we find ourselves in a contest in which our opponent is quite vocal, we can either fight fire with fire, or choose to ignore him. *In either case our goal is to <u>remain undisturbed</u> so that we may continue to perform at our optimum level.*

If we choose to ignore him, our best plan is to remember the detriment of a cumbersome ego, and simply dismiss such silly superficial nudging. Besides, the final laugh is always found on the scoreboard. If we play our game, our opponent will eventually grow wary of expending so much energy in vain, and he will quiet down.

If we do find ourselves becoming intimidated at our opponent's apparent confidence, we must remedy the situation at once. A simple solution is to boldly affirm out loud how much better we are than he. This is not so much for him to hear as it is for us. Such self-affirmation is quite effective in stabilizing confidence. If we believe in our heart what we say, and let ourselves hear it, our play will follow accordingly.

## *Mum's The Word*

It is very important that we keep our understanding under lock and key, for the surrender of our secrets will yield many of them sterile. While at the end of the series we may feel the urge to triumphantly show our friend the different strategies and techniques we have been employing, we must remember the elimination of the ego and have restraint if they are to work in the future.

# CONCLUSION

We have come a long way. While it may have appeared that blitz chess was merely a standard game of chess played within a smaller time interval, we have now witnessed that this is far from the truth. The time crisis creates a whole new arena in which the successful strategies originate from a well-tempered synthesis of the board logic and time meter.

The most wide reaching aspect of this new system is the advocation of a tactical approach over a positional one. The positional player no longer has the time to administer delicate refutations to spirited attempts at complications. Because of this, tactics decide the winner; thus, the best blitz players are tacticians.

This leads to an opening repertoire designed for the greatest tactical chances. Since our opponent does not have time to ponder positions new to him, outstanding consideration is also given to the novelty and rarity of our openings.

Through active manipulation of the time crisis, we transform it into a potent tool. By moving rapidly, initiating bluffs, and adapting to escalating blitz peril, our play integrates not only logic but a massive psychological ideology characteristic to champion blitz competition. To top it off, we also have a formidable arsenal of specific blitz traps that snare even the most experienced gladiators.

All this considered, the unwary opponent doesn't stand a chance with a gameplan of mere chess theory. Expecting a placid, enduring journey, he will be devoured in short order by the ensuing ten-minute tempest. He will have no idea what hit him, for while he plays chess, we play blitz. Go get 'em!

# EXERCISES

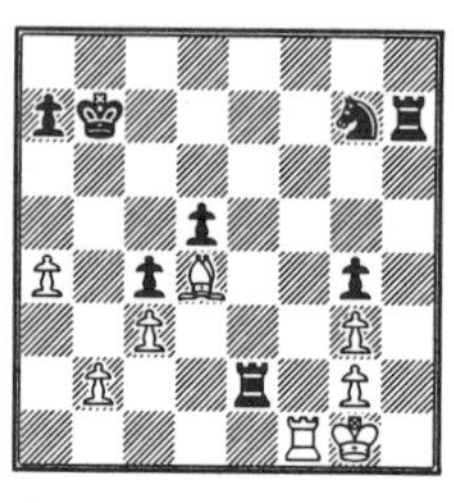

0:18

0:13

1.

3:58

4:05

2.

0:04

0:07

3.

1:31

1:43

4.

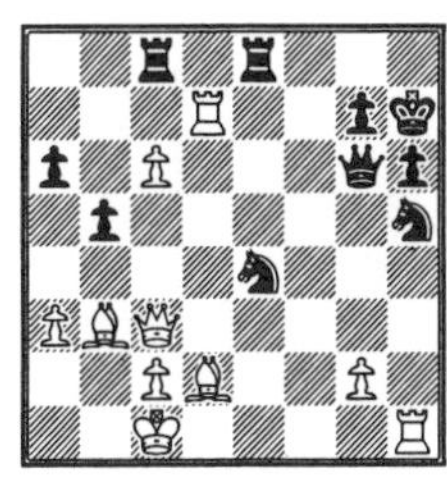

0:12

0:10

**5.**

1:40

2:02

**6.**

1:25

1:52

**7.**

3:17

2:59

**8.**

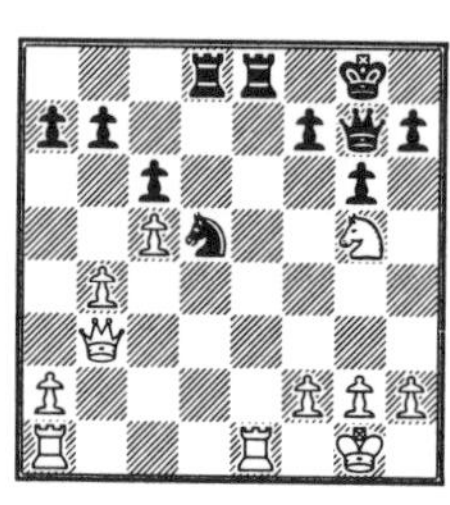

2:00

2:11

9.

0:03

0:03

10.

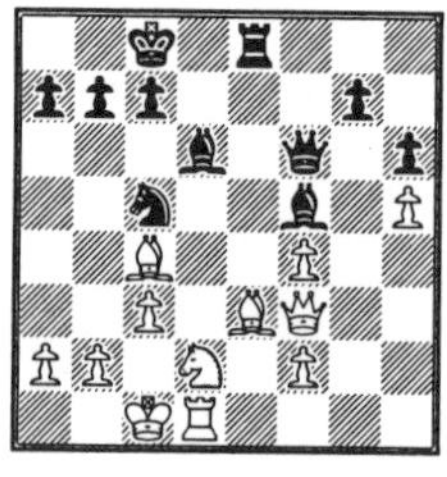

2:06

2:32

11.

0:14

0:08

12.

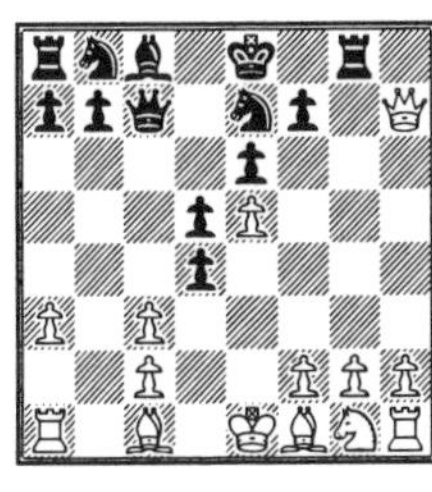

4:35

4:31

13.

0:08

0:04

14.

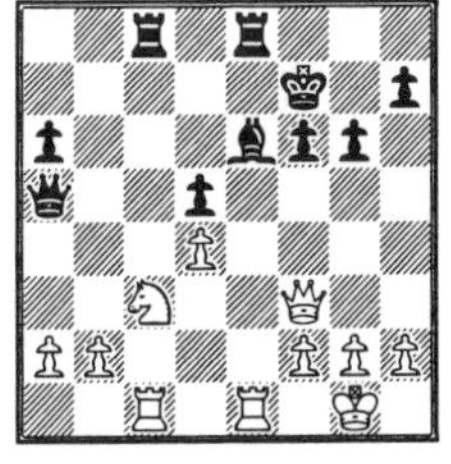

3:07

2:51

15.

2:14

2:57

16.

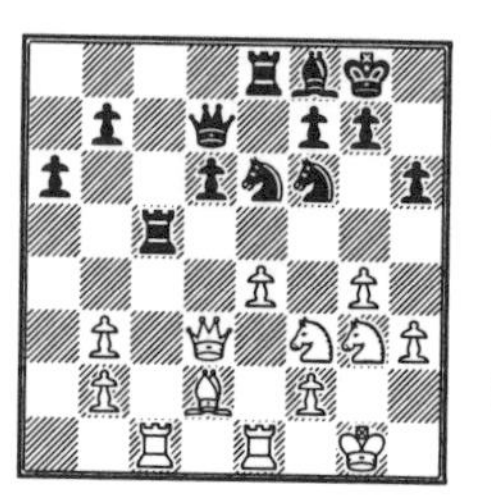

0:22

0:13

17.

2:45

2:28

18.

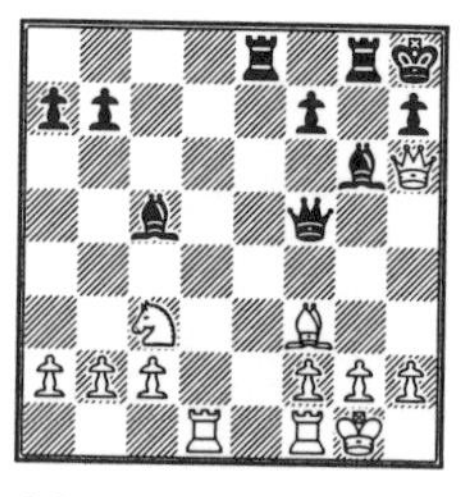

1:50

1:51

19.

1:23

1:06

20.

# SOLUTIONS

## *Basic Tactics p.38 - 41*

1. Qa7
2. Qxh...KxQ, hg...Kxg, Be4#
3. Bc5...Bb6, Qf4
4. Rg8
5. Qxh+...QxQ, BxQ+...KxB, RxR
6. Bf5...Kd8, RxN...cxR, c6
7. Ng4
8. Qh8+...KxQ, Bf6+...Kg8, Rd8#
9. f7+
10. Nxp+...dxN, d5
11. Qe5
12. Rc6+...Bc6, Nc5+...Ka5, Bc7#
13. Ne5
14. Qxh+...KxQ, Ng5+...Kh6, Nxf7+ Draw
15. Ng5
16. Be7

## *Blitz Exercises*

1. Rf6 "check"
2. Nxe sacrifice (Bxe is also ok)
3. Kg1 closest to clock
4. Qc7??!
5. Qxp stunning
6. h3 luft
7. Kf2 (nothing special warranted)
8. Kb1 diffusing skewer threat
9. h3 luft
10. Kf4 closest to clock
11. Bd4 diffusing mating combinations
12. Rg7 "check"
13. Kd1 diffusing fork threat (not Ne2)
14. h4 closest to clock
15. h3 luft
16. Rxh sacrifice
17. Kh2 keeping position complicated
18. Ne4 (nothing special warranted)
19. Kh1 diffusing tactics
20. Bd4??!